HINDU FEASTS FASTS AND CEREMONIES

S. M. Natesa Sastri

HINDU FEASTS FASTS AND CEREMONIES

Pt. S.M. Natesa Sastri

WITH AN INTRODUCTION BY
HENRY K. BEAUCHAMP

GYAN

Published by

GYAN

Gyan Publishing House
5, Ansari Road
Daryaganj, New Delhi-110002
Phone: 011-47034999, 9811692060
E-mail: books@gyanbooks.com

Distribution Network
gyanbooks.com
India, USA, Canada, UK, Australia, France

ISBN : 978-81-212-3479-5 (PB)
First Published, 1903

2nd Impression 2020

Printed at: Gyan Press, Delhi.

Hindu Feasts Fasts and Ceremonies
Author: Pt. S.M. Natesa Sastri

INTRODUCTION

THE work which Pandit Natesa Sastri has been engaged in for so many years, and of which this volume is only one small exemplar, deserves every welcome and support, as much from his own countrymen as from foreign dwellers in the land. The folklore of a country is never so well known even by the folk of the country itself, that popular literature concerning it is not to be heartily welcomed. Moreover there is always a young generation growing up which is waiting to be instructed in it by the easiest and widest possible means.

The simpler tenets of religion and the more popular tales and legends are learned from the lips of parents and teachers: but there is much that can only be learned from books. Further, in these days of hurry and stress, by which even India is being more or less affected, the old leisurely, yet possibly more thorough, methods of oral tradition and teaching are no longer possible, and we must trust more and more to written and printed records. Pandit Natesa Sastri is doing most excellent work in collecting, arranging and recording in concise and easily assimilable form some of the more noticeable tales, traditions, customs, beliefs, and ceremonies of the Hindus. And it is to be hoped that many others of his educated fellow-countrymen will follow his good example. For there are mines of wealth to be exploited in this manner, and there is work for many scores of writers, compilers and translators.

There is no country in the world, moreover, where such studies are of more importance than in India, for with the Hindu, customs and traditions explain almost every act of his every-day life. As a learned writer on the Hindus has well said :—" With the Hindu, religion is not a thing for times and seasons only, but professes to regulate his life in its many relations. It orders ceremonies to be performed on his behalf before he is born, and others after his death. It ordains those attendant on his birth, his early training, his food, his style of dress and its manufacture, his employment, marriage, amusements. It seeks to regulate not only his private life, but also his domestic and national. To treat of the ordinary life of the Hindu is to describe his religion."

It follows from this that for Hindus to know themselves, or for others to know them, a study of such matters as Pandit Natesa Sastri sets forth in this little book, as in others of his writings, is essential.

At the same time there is one point that must ever be kept in mind, namely the danger of generalising with regard to Hindu manners, customs, ceremonies and traditions. As the writer above quoted remarks :—" It should be remembered that descriptions true of certain classes or of certain districts may not be correct of other classes or other districts; and that frequently the residents of one district are totally ignorant of what prevails in others. This can scarcely be wondered at when we consider the number of books which are accepted by the people as divinely given for authorities concerning the gods and the religious life. The people of one district are familiar with only a small part of one book, whilst those of other districts found their faiths on other books or different parts of the same. In addition to this it must not be forgotten that a century ago there was no prose literature, no newspapers, magazines, or novels; whilst the theatrical representations were almost entirely confined to mythological subjects. It is no uncommon thing to find a custom in the home, or a ceremony in worship, supported by quite different authorities by different people."

It is one of the excellent characteristics of Pandit Natesa Sastri that he particularises where necessary and generalises only where it is safe to do so.

It seems hardly necessary to point out or emphasise how specially valuable to foreign students are Pandit Natesa Sastri's works, and others similar to them. The bounden duty laid upon all Europeans living in this country and earning their livelihood in it, of striving to understand and appreciate the people among whom they dwell, needs no argument or demonstration. Such knowledge and appreciation cannot be acquired without careful study and observation. But now-a-days, at any rate, he who runs may read many excellent treatises both by natives of India and by Europeans on various aspects and characteristics of Hinduism and the Hindus; and for a general work-a-day knowledge of the Hindus there is no more useful, and at the same time more interesting, study than that of current beliefs and practices such as are described by Pandit Natesa Sastri in this little volume.

HENRY BEAUCHAMP.

MADRAS,
9th December, 1902.

CONTENTS

Hindu Feasts, Fasts and Ceremonies

1. The Ardra

THE followers of the Saiva religion deem five places in Southern India most holy, and they are:—Conjeeveram, where Siva is worshipped in the shape of *Prithvi-linga* or as the representative of the element earth; Tiruvanaikovil, near Trichinopoly, where he is worshipped in the shape of water-*linga*; Sri Kalahasti, the shrine containing the air-*linga*; Tiruvannamalai, the seat of the fire-*linga*; and Chidambaram, the abode of the ether-*linga*. The several forms of the god Siva in these sacred shrines are considered to be the bodies or casements of the soul whose natural bases are the five elements—earth, water, fire, air and ether. The apprehension of God in the last of these five as ether is, according to the Saiva school of philosophy, the highest form of worship, for, it is not the worship of God in a tangible form, but the worship of what, to ordinary minds, is vacuum, which nevertheless leads to the attainment of a knowledge of the all-pervading without physical accessories in the shape of any *linga*, which is, after all, an emblem. That this is the case at Chidambaram is known to every Hindu, for if he ever asks the priests to show him the God in the temple he is pointed to an empty space in the most holy of the holies, which has been termed the *Akasa*, or ether-*linga*. In this lies the so-called *Chidambara-rahasya*—the secret of worship in the sacred city of Chidambaram. When any devotee has reached the stage of worshipping God in this manner, he is, according to the Saiva doctrine, deemed to be exempt from all future births and is supposed to secure absorption in the supreme essence of God. It is on account of this high nature of worship that the main hall of the Siva temple in this town is termed the *chit-sabha*—the hall in which the true devotee acquires illimitable and supernatural powers which could be obtained only by concentrated devotion to God and which when once acquired could be exercised at pleasure. Including the *chit-sabha*—the hall of supreme vision and wisdom, there are five chief halls in the Chidambaram shrine, which are called the *kanaka-sabha*—the golden hall; the *chitra-sabha*—ornamental hall; the *deva-sabha*—the divine hall; and the *nritta-sabha*—the hall of dancing. The special deity worshipped in the temple is called Natesa—the lord of dancers. His other names are *Nataraja*—the king of dancers; *Sabhesa*—the lord of the several sacred halls; and *Sabhapati*—the president of these sacred halls. The prominent idea underlying the *Sthala Purana* of Chidambaram is that the great God having perceived his own Self in Himself is illuminated with wisdom and dances with very joy on account thereof; and that the devotee who visits the temple and witnesses this dance becomes himself absorbed in God. The Chidambaram shrine has thus from time immemorial been a visible symbol of a philosophic phase of the Hindu religion. It is the place where, according to Hindu beliefs, persons even of the lowest caste have attained oneness with God by sincere devotion and faith. Nanda—a Paraiya saint—attained eternal felicity by his devotions at Chidambaram. The most orthodox of the orthodox Brahmans will never stint the reputation of this greatest of Saiva saints, who after all was only a Paraiya by birth. It is the only place in the whole of India where no attempt has been made to import conventional ideas of Godhead into the purely philosophic basis of the Hindu religion. In keeping with this fame, Chidambaram is now the seat of several Sudra monasteries, where several hundreds of Sudra mendicants are taught Sanskrit. A Brahman visitor to this sacred town will be surprised to see the number of Sudras repeating the *Upanishads* in the early morning in these monasteries. To add to his wonder he will find that they have not only got by heart these sacred writings but that they understand their meaning and possess a perfect knowledge of the subject-matter which is a rare thing even with Brahmans.

Such is the merit of Chidambaram. Special meritoriousness is attached by the Saivites to the Ardra festival which takes place in this town on the full-moon day of the month of

Margasira, according to the Hindu year,—corresponding to the latter half of December and the first half of January. As the Hindu deity Rama is supposed to have been born on a *Navami* day and Krishna on an *Ashtami* day, so Siva in his incarnation of Natesa is considered by the Saivites to have been born on the full-moon day of the month of Margasira and in the constellation of Ardra—the sixth lunar mansion. On the night previous to the feast the bathing of the image of the god Natesa takes place on a grand scale. Of the Hindu trinity Siva is supposed to be fond of baths and Vishnu of ornaments. The Siva god of Chidambaram—lord Natesa—is bathed only six times in a year, and the bath on the night previous to the Ardra feast is conducted on the grandest scale. Pilgrims and devotees flock to the hall where this bathing is performed. Pots full of milk, honey, lemon-juice, pomegranate juice, cocoanut water, ghee, oil, sandal paste, curds, holy ashes, and other liquids and solids, considered as sacred offerings to the deity, pour in from all parts to be used on the occasion. This ceremony commences at about midnight and lasts till late in the morning. When the bathing is over the image is choicely decorated; and the Brahman priests of Chidambaram are considered to be adepts at showing off the image to its best advantage. The decoration is done behind screens and when the screens are raised the whole hall rings with the hymns of praise chanted by the thousands of pilgrims and devotees who have assembled there to worship God. The choicest temple jewels in southern India, made of the finest of precious stones, are to be seen only in two shrines—Srirangam and Chidambaram. Natesa on the Ardra festival day is most superbly decorated and at about evening time is taken round on a grand procession. This is the most impressive scene of the Ardra festival and the *Anandatandavam* —the dance in ecstatic joy—takes place on this occasion. The bearers of the image have a mode of marching slowly, so as to give the image the appearance of dancing. The most holy of holies—the *Garbhagriha* of the temple—is reached after a slow march of three or four hours; and this completes the Ardra feast.

There is a queer story in connection with this feast which obtains credence with the mass of the worshippers, but which is not to be found in any of the Hindu Puranas. It is that the god Siva left his inner apartments one night and returned home early next morning. The goddess Parvati grew jealous on this account and denied him admission. Hot words were exchanged and soon after reconciliation followed. In keeping with this legend the temple doors are shut just as the god enters at the close of the procession on the Ardra day, and questions and replies take place between two priests who represent the god and goddess. After the supposed reconciliation the doors are opened. This, as has been said already, is entirely a popular belief, having no Puranic foundation.

The places in Southern India most sacred to this feast are Chidambaram in the South Arcot District, Tiruvalur in the Tanjore District, Lalgudi in the Trichinopoly District, and Perur in the Coimbatore District. The great Saiva philosopher—Manikkavasakar—passed his latter days in Chidambaram and worshipped Natesa. A small festival in honour of the memory of this philosopher takes place on this occasion in the temple.

2. Avani Avittam

UPAKARMA, or *Avani Avittam*, as it is called in Tamil, is a holy day with the twice-born castes, especially the Brahmans. It always falls on the day when the moon is in the asterism of *Sravishtha* in the fifth lunar month of *Avani*—July and August. It is the day of the annual renewal of the sacred thread of the twice-born castes,—Brahmans, Kshatriyas and Vaisyas. The daily rites of a Brahman are several and every Brahman must, properly speaking, go through every one of these rites, though the rule now is more honoured in the breach than in the observance. The rites are as follows :—

A Brahman, as soon as he rises from his bed, must clean his teeth with the twig of the Ficus Racemosa (fig tree) or mango leaf. He must then rinse his mouth twelve times with water. He must then proceed to bathe in a river or in other water and pray before bathing. After bathing the Brahman has put on his clean apparel. He must then wash his hands and feet and sip water thrice in the name of Maha Vishnu. He must perform his morning worship—*pratah sandhya*—with *arghya*—oblations of water—and *gayatri*—meditation on the Sun-god. After this the Brahman must proceed to study the *Vedas* under his preceptor—*guru*. A portion of this sacred lore is got up by heart every day. The *guru*—teacher—sits facing the east and recites the text and the student sits facing the west and repeats the same. This practice must be gone through daily till the whole of the *Vedas* is learnt by heart. This continues till midday. The *Vedas*, *Upanishads*, codes of law and other branches of sacred literature must be gone through thus and acquired by the Brahman.

Then the midday bathing and prayers succeed, followed by the worship of the Manes. Water with sesamum seeds is offered as an oblation to the Manes, from the hollow of both hands joined. After the propitiation of the Manes, the propitiation of the deities commences, which consists of oblations of fire with prayers addressed to several gods. After finishing this the Brahman goes to his midday meal. Before, however, sitting down for his dinner he is ordained to see whether any guests are waiting at his door; and if so, he must receive them, present them with planks to sit on, give them water for ablution, and offer them honey mixed with other food for refreshment. He must then take them into his house and feed them sumptuously. The evening closes with bath and prayers as in the morning. These, then, form the daily routine of a Brahman. But few observe them regularly, and those too are to be found in remote villages. Even they become liable to lapses from the daily routine.

Upakarma or *Avani Avittam* was instituted at a very distant epoch of time for those that had not attended regularly to the performance of these rites and for those who, though regular, had deviated on certain occasions during the year. Thus the day of *Upakarma* is the annual renewal day of the sacred thread—the symbol of the obligations of the twice-born—of the Brahmans and other twice-born castes. Early in the morning of this day every Brahman who is invested with the holy thread bathes and offers his usual morning prayers. After these are over, and as a preparatory rite to the *Avani Avittam* or *Sravani* ceremony, he repeats the *Kamokarshit* prayer. This prayer affirms that for each individual who recites it, all his sins of omission, commission and deviation originated from anger or passion, and that his soul which is by nature pure is not responsible for them. This prayer he repeats a hundred and eight times. This is the morning ceremony on the *Sravani* day. The ceremony proper commences at about midday. At that time all the Brahmans assemble and go in a body to the river or sacred tank of the village or town in which they live. The priest dictates to them a *Sankalpa* praying that the effect of all the sins that they have committed either consciously or unconsciously may perish with their plunge in the holy water; and consecrating the water each performs his bathing. This ceremony takes from an hour to an hour and a half. After bath the new sacred thread is worn and the old one is removed and cast away. This means that the Brahman commences his religious life anew from the *Sravani* day. All the ceremonies connected with the investiture of the sacred thread—*upanayana*—are performed on a small scale on this day. A commencement is made of the study of the *Vedas*, *Upanishads*, codes of law and other departments of knowledge. Each lore is in turn taken up and finished. The first sentence and the last sentence of an Upanishad are repeated, and this act performed on the *Sravani* day means that the subject to which the sentences refer has been commenced and finished. The propitiation of the Manes by the offerings of water and sesamum and of the gods by oblations of ghee in the fire finish the *Sravani* ceremony. A good and sumptuous afternoon dinner follows and closes the ceremonies of the day.

Thus with the renewal of his sacred thread, the Brahman renews his sacred studies also. All his deviations from established rules having been rightly traced to either passion or anger, he confesses in a general way his sins, promises to cast them off from the *Sravani* day, recommences all the various departments of the study of Sanskrit lore, commences and finishes the *Vedas* themselves and becomes in every sense, as the ceremony at least declares him to be, a pure Brahman again. On this special account the *Sravani* is also termed the *Upakarma*—the commencement of the study of the *Vedas*. This *Sravani* ceremony is a most ancient one and is coeval with the civilisation of the Brahmans. The Rigveda Brahmans perhaps instituted it and the Yajurveda Brahmans followed it. It is not a Puranic rite but a rite sanctioned by the *Vedas* themselves. It is therefore one of the oldest rites of the Brahmans.

The *gayatri* day is a day of prayer performed on the day next to the *Sravani* day. The *Gayatri* is a sacred verse repeated by every Brahman at his morning, midday and evening devotions and on other occasions also. Great sins are believed to be expiated by a pious repetition of this verse. The general meaning of the verse is as follows :—" Let us contemplate the divine splendour of the Sun-God, the donor of bliss to all, that he may give us all kinds of happiness in all the worlds."

Every Brahman is required to repeat the *gayatri* at least thirty-two times each time—morning, midday and evening. This makes it obligatory on every religious Brahman to meditate on the *gayatri* at least ninety-six times every day. But there might have been days in the year on which a Brahman was not able to observe this. To make amends for all the shortcomings, the *gayatri* is repeated 1,008 times on the day succeeding the *Sravani* day, and hence the day next to the *Sravani* is called the day of the *gayatri japa*. It takes generally four to five hours to pronounce the incantation 1,008 times and this number must be reached before midday.

The Brahmans, as a class, attach the greatest importance to these two—the *Sravani* and the *Gayatri*—days.

3. The Mahalaya Amavasa

AMAVÁSA, or the day of the conjunction of the sun and the moon, occurs once every month and it is a day considered by the Hindus to be specially set apart for the offering of oblations and the performance of religious ceremonies to the *Pitris* or the spirits of departed ancestors. Such being the general belief, what is the reason for the Hindus paying greater attention to the Mahalaya Amavasa, or the new moon day of the month of *Kanya* (Tamil *Purattasi*) when the sun is in the sign *Virgo*? The *Itihasa*, a great authority on the religious rites of the Hindus, says that the moment the sun enters the sign *Virgo* (*Kanya*) the departed Manes, leaving their abode in the world of Yama, the Destroyer, come down to the world of man and occupy the houses of their descendants in this world or as it is said in Sanskrit, *Kanya yate yatha surye pitaras tishtanti sve grihe.* Therefore the fortnight preceding the new moon of the month of *Kanya* is considered as the fortnight which is specially sacred to the propitiation of the Manes or departed spirits. *Dine dine gaya tulyam*—The ceremonies in honour of the Manes performed during each day of this fortnight are considered to be equal to the ceremonies performed in the sacred city of Gaya. But instead of performing these rites on each of the days or the fortnight, most Hindus do so only on one of the days. Orthodox Hindus, however, perform ceremonies on every one of the days of this fortnight. These ceremonies terminate on the Mahalaya Amavasa day, which is therefore observed with greater sanctity than other new moon days. If, through unavoidable causes, any Hindu is not able to perform his Mahalaya rites during the course of the fortnight preceding the Mahalaya Amavasa, he is allowed as a concession to perform the same in the fortnight succeeding this new moon, because it is said that the Manes continue to linger in his house, expecting him to perform the ceremonies, till the sun enters the sign *Scorpio* (*Vichchhika*), *i. e.*, till about the next full moon day. If even by that time a Hindu has not performed these ceremonies to the

Manes they are said to become disgusted with him and return to the world of Yama after cursing their descendants in this world. *Vrichchhika darsanat yanti nirasa pitaro gatah.*

Such is the belief about the Mahalaya Amavasa and the two lunar fortnights which precede and succeed it. The month of *Kanya* is thus reserved for the worship of departed spirits and the most propitious portion of the month for such worship is the fortnight preceding the Mahalaya Amavasa. Generally speaking, every Hindu strictly observes his Mahalaya. If he is careless about it, he will find it difficult to have a peaceful time with the old ladies in his house.

4. The Bhogi and the Pongal

THE Tamil month of Margali (Sans. *Mrigasira*), corresponding mostly with December and running on to the 11th January, is considered by the Hindus to be a most unhealthy month. It is the month in which all kinds of epidemics—cholera, fever and small-pox are supposed to occur. Accordingly, the last day of this Tamil month is observed as a festive day by the Hindus in Southern India in thankfulness to the higher powers that the worst month has ended. The feast is called the *Bhogi-Pandigai* or feast in honour of Indra, the king of heavens, the lord of the clouds, rain, seasons and everything that is the source of happiness and plenty. The word *Bhoga* comes from the Sanskrit root *Bhuj*, to enjoy. So *Bhogi-Pandigai* is a feast of enjoyment on account of deliverance from the calamitous month of *Mrigasira*.

Pongal or *Sankramana* or *Sankranti* is a festival which is observed on the first day of the Tamil month of *Tai* (Sans. *Makara*). It is a New Year's day astronomically, and commences approximately on the 12th January every year. It is observed by the Hindus by offering boiled rice in milk to propitiate the Sun-god. Hence the feast is called the *Pongal*, which in Tamil means boiled rice. This feast is also called the Uttarayana feast, as the sun commences his journey towards the North on this day. Sankranti or Sankramana, which is the Aryan name for the Pongal, means the entrance of the sun into the sign Capricorn.

The *Pongal* is observed as a day for the special worship of the sun throughout India by the Hindus. Everything sweet is supposed to please the sun-god. So rice with sugar and milk is cooked on this day in every Hindu household. The sun-god is worshipped in the courtyard of the house with diagrams in red mud describing the sun and the moon, and *puja* is performed on a large scale. The Pongal food, which consists of sugar-cane and sugar-candy forms the chief offering to the god. This also constitutes the first course in a Hindu dinner. Rich men regard this day as a meritorious one for making charitable donations, and every

Hindu Raja gives away large sums in charity. An assembly of Pandits sits on this day in Baroda, and grants rewards to the Hindu scholars who have passed examinations in the several departments of the *Vedas*, *Tarka*, *Vyakarana*, etc., of the Sanskrit language. Other Native Courts also observe the same custom. The season for marriages in Hindu households also commences on this day and lasts for six months up to the end of the *Uttarayana*—the whole of the summer solstice. The brides for the year get their presents on the *Sankranti* day and these are called the *Sankranti Siru*. They consist generally of new cloths, one or two ornaments and vessels and also sugar-canes, molasses, oil, ghee, etc. The *Sankranti* is also the day of the year in which all the old earthen utensils of a Hindu household are replaced by new ones. The *pongal*—boiled rice—itself must be cooked in a new pot.

The day after the *Pongal* is called the *Mattupongal* feast, or the feast in honour of the cattle. On this day all the cows, bullocks, buffaloes and horses in a Hindu household are well washed and decorated. They are also worshipped, and cooked rice is given to them. Cows generally eat cooked rice freely but bullocks and horses will not as a rule. Towards evening festoons of aloe fibre and cloths containing coins are tied to the horns of bullocks and cows and the animals are driven through the streets with tom-tom and music. This ceremony is not much observed in populous towns or by the Brahmans. They merely worship the cow during the day time. But in the villages, especially in villages inhabited by the Kalla or robber tribes, the maiden chooses as her husband him who has safely untied and brought to her the cloth tied to the horn of the fiercest bull. The bullocks are let loose with their horns carrying valuables amidst the din of tom-tom and harsh music which terrify and bewilder them. They run madly about and are purposely excited by the crowd. A young Kalla will declare that he will run after such and such a bullock—and this is sometimes a risky pursuit—and recover the valuables tied to its horn, and he does so often in a dexterous manner. These *tamashas* take place on a grand scale in villages round about Madura and Tinnevelly where Kallas live in large numbers.

Accidents are very common but they are not allowed to interfere with the festivities. Besides, the Kalla considers it a great disgrace to be injured while chasing a bull.

5. The Dipavali

ON the day of the *Dipavali* feast every Hindu gets up at about 4 o'clock in the morning and bathes in oil before sunrise. From the baby to the oldest member in every Hindu household—every male and female—has to go through this oil bath before sunrise—for the meritoriousness (*punya*) of the bath is supposed to be lost if it is not undergone before the appearance of the Lord of the day. What is the origin of this bath and why is so much sanctity attached to it? The *Dipavali* too is only of *puranic* sanction. The legend or legends which are quoted for the observance of this feast are to be found in the *Bhagavata*. At the time of Sri Krishna there was a mighty demon, named Narakasura, reigning over the country, called Pragjyotisha—the district lying to the east of Bengal, probably the western portion of Assam. According to a certain story Narakasura carried off the earnings of Aditi, the mother of the gods. The gods were powerless to recover the jewels and applied to Sri Krishna for help. Krishna fought with the demon, slew him and brought back the jewels. Another story says that Narakasura assumed the shape of an elephant and carried off the daughter of Visvakarma—the architect of the gods—and outraged her. He also seized the best daughters of the Gandharva (demi-gods) gods, and men and the divine nymphs themselves and made for himself a harem of 16,000 beautiful damsels. During his reign no woman considered herself secure, and so all joined together and petitioned Vishnu to destroy the demon and thus put an end to his atrocities. But with all his vices Narakasura had accumulated such a vast fund of meritoriousness by his penances and contemplation at the commencement of his career that Vishnu for a long time condones his crimes, till at last, unable any more to bear his havocs, allowed Sri Krishna to march to Pragjyotisha and slay him. In his last moments Narakasura came to his senses, praised the deity for his having come down in the incarnation of Sri Krishna to give him eternal felicity (*moksha*) and began to repent of his immoral life. As he was always a gay person revelling in worldly pleasures, feasts, baths, women, display of fireworks, etc., he requested the great god that the day of his death (*moksha*) should be honoured by the Hindus in revels and festivities. "Let it be so" said Sri Krishna and transferred the 16,000 damsels collected by Narakasura from Pragjyotisha to his own harem at Dvaraka, where they, after a certain time, became *Rishis* or sages.

So, the *Dipavali* goes by another name of the *Narakachaturdasi*, *i.e.*, the fourteenth day of the dark fortnight of the month of *Tula* (October—November) on which the demon Narakasura was put to death by Sri Krishna. And the Hindus consider the oil bath in the morning of that day before sunrise equal to a bath in the sacred waters of the holy Ganges. After the bath in the early morning every Hindu takes a small quantity of a special medicine which is prepared for the occasion, and which is mostly composed of ginger powder. Then every male who can afford the cost wears a pair of new *dhoties*. The females and children have also their *saris* and *bachkana* cloths. A light refreshment of sweetmeats and fruits is then taken by every one and the children and youngsters go to fire crackers on a large scale. The elder members again bathe after 6 A.M. and proceed to the temple (if there is one near) to worship the God. Then relatives and friends living near are visited. Every Hindu who meets another asks him "Have you had the holy Ganges bath?" "Yes, Sir, by the favour of your blessing" is the reply. At the end of every visit to a house *pan supari* is distributed. At midday a sumptuous dinner closes the *Dipavali* festivities. The *Dipavali* is observed, in the Tamil, Telugu and Kanarese Districts of the Madras Presidency as a feast set apart for wearing new cloths. Men, women and children from the highest to the lowest wear new cloths on this day. But if any calamity, such as the death of a near or dear relative, has visited any family within a year, the observance of the *Dipavali* is given up that year in that family. Mourning in Hindu societies is observed for one year, and a house which is in mourning does not keep up festivities for that period. This is the universal rule. In such houses there would not be oil baths or wearing new apparel or exchange of visits, or congratulations for the holy Ganges baths. But even such houses freely give permission to their youngsters to indulge in crackers, for the mirth of children should not be curtailed. In Madras the wearing of the new apparel is done during the *Krittika* feast by the non-Brahman population.

There is a certain Hindu saying to the effect that "toddy a thousand years old will be drained on the *Dipavali.*" This is too true with the low and poorer class of the Hindus, and especially the labourers. They make this the greatest drinking day of the year. Children enjoy the *Dipavali* feast the most. With them this feast is only for spending as much money as possible in harmless fireworks. The genius of European merchants has invented so many varieties of crackers and gay lights of fancy colours and these with the Chinese crackers are bought to a very large extent and lighted up or fired as the case may be. Even the poorest household spends a couple of rupees at least in providing these enjoyments to its youngsters. Rich men, not to speak of Zamindars, buy for hundreds and thousands and a very large amount of money which could be better utilised is wasted on this day—in smoke, as an ironical Tamil proverb very well puts it, *Kasai Kariyakkade banam vangi sudu*—"Do not waste your money, buy crackers and fire them." Pipers and drummers visit every house which celebrates this feast at about 3 in the morning and play upon their instruments for a few minutes and go away. This is of course a convenient arrangement to awake the inmates in time. But they turn up again in the morning to demand presents; the peons, the house servants, the sweeper and the scavenger, where these exist, must have their *bakshis* on this day. These are minor indents on one's purse which is, however, easily and gladly managed. But the major indents are the costly presents to the bride or bridegroom as the case may be. The bride's parents invite the bridegroom or *vice versa* and in addition to presenting him with costly cloths according to the position and wealth of the party, they have also to give costly presents in the shape of jewels and vessels to which a large quantity of gingelly oil, fruits and other sundries are also added. This is generally done on the first *Dipavali* after the marriage, once by the bride's family and a second time by that of the bridegroom, but the presentation of cloth or cloths continues as long as the relationship continues. In Northern India and among the Gujaratis of Madras, the *Dipavali* is the day of the closing of the annual accounts. From this day new accounts are opened in newly-bound account books, and this continues till the *Dipavali* of the next year, when fresh accounts are again opened.

The word *Dipavali* is a Sanskrit compound, made up of two simple words, *Dipa*, meaning lights, and *avali*, a row, thus a row of lights. The feast is purely an Aryan one. In Madras we do not notice any row of lights on the night of the *Dipavali* or on the preceding night in front of houses; to a small extent we observe this display on the *Krittika* day. But in Northern India, Bombay and Bengal the literal meaning of the word *Dipavali* is well carried out in the observance of this feast, and one's eyes are almost dazzled by the rows of lights displayed in the fronts of houses in exceedingly fanciful arrangements. Thanks also to the invention of gas lights, every Hindu or Parsee merchant in Bombay spends hundreds of rupees in conducting gas to the front of his house and laying thousands and ten thousands of lights there. If any one cares to enjoy the *Dipavali* he should be in Bombay to witness this feast.

6. The Hindus and the Eclipse

THE Hindus were the first to have correct and scientific ideas about eclipses. Varahamihira, the greatest Hindu astronomer, who flourished in the sixth century A.D., has described the phenomena of eclipses in the same way as any astronomer of the twentieth century would do. But with the generality of the Hindus the eclipse is the swallowing of the sun and the moon for a time by a demon called Rahu. Rahu is also one of the nine planets in the astronomy of the Hindus, the ascending node. If any Hindu calendar is consulted for the figure of an eclipse, Rahu, in the form of a monstrous serpent or dragon, will be seen to grasp the sun. Thus the common Hindu believes the eclipse to be a great calamity that has come over the luminaries. He has to fast for six hours before the commencement of the eclipse, and prepares his food and eats only after the eclipse is over. During the course of the eclipse he has to perform certain ceremonies. As soon as the first contact takes place he bathes and offers prayers to the Manes. After the last phase of the eclipse he bathes again, offers certain prayers and returns home. During the course of the eclipse he stays by the side of a river or on the sea-shore. River-baths and sea-baths are performed on this occasion to propitiate the Manes. Some devout Hindus go on a pilgrimage to Rameswaram or Benares to plunge themselves in the waters of the ocean or the Ganges during the eclipse.

The eclipse must take place on some asterism or other, and if that asterism happens to be that in which any Hindu was born, he has to perform some special ceremonies to absolve himself from impending evil. Every Hindu who was born in the asterism in which the eclipse takes place considers it as foreboding some calamity for him in that year. He makes a plate of gold or silver or of palm-leaf, according to his means, and ties it on his forehead, with Sanskrit verses inscribed over it. He sits with this plate for some time, performs certain ceremonies, bathes with the plate untied and presents it to a Brahman with some fee, ranging from four annas to several thousands of rupees, according to his means. Maharajahs give large donations to Brahmans on this occasion. Nearly 90 per cent. of the copper-plate grants of the Vijayanagar period of the 15th and 16th centuries A. D. are donations of villages and of property to Brahmans by the Hindu kings of Vijayanagar on the occasions of either a solar or a lunar eclipse. Even now in Travancore, Mysore, Baroda and other Native States, the Brahmans are most munificently remunerated on eclipse occasions.

The belief that an eclipse is a calamity to the sun or the moon is such a strong Hindu belief that no marriages take place in the months in which an eclipse falls. Even the most educated Hindu who has taken his degree, with special distinction in astronomy probably, undergoes all the Hindu rites on the occasion. The eclipse time is considered a most auspicious time for mastering the incantations for exorcising the evil effects of serpent bite, or scorpion-sting, and of devils, and many specialists in these directions would be seen standing in water and muttering these incantations.

7. Hindu Funeral Rites

A Hindu funeral, as it is now performed, has undergone many changes from what it was originally meant by the ancient sages of India to be, and as such deserves handling in a critical way. Every religion has its own mode of conducting its funeral rites. The Hindu mode is that the son or the sons or the nearest agnatic kindred must perform these parting ceremonies. As soon as all hope of life is given up, the family priest summons all the sons to sit by the side of the dying father. To avoid confusion, let us suppose the dying party to be the father, and that his sons perform the rites. Certain donations are first given to the Brahmans. A lighted lamp, a vessel full of sesamum seed, a vessel filled with oil, a milch cow with its calf —these four must be given, or if a person is too poor to buy a cow, he must at least give a couple of rupees. These donations are considered to be most effective in washing away the sins of the dying man; and, as a corollary, he who receives the gifts is supposed to inherit the sins of the dying person. Hence it is very difficult to find persons to receive the donations voluntarily; and to induce the acceptance of them, large fees have sometimes to be offered. The men who accept the bribes are Brahmans of very inferior social scale, who appear with hideous faces, which proclaim that the average lustre of their caste has left them long ago. Then succeeds the sacred bath to purify the soul and atone for the sins of the dying person —it is called the *Kaveri* or *samudra snana*, as the person dying happens to be near a river or the sea—and fees are paid to Brahmans, who are supposed to perform the ablutions. The fee for each bath is generally six annas and a quarter. In rich families fees are given for a thousand such baths. As it is considered very respectable to receive this kind of fee, a good number of high class Brahmans is always available for this purpose.

After giving the gifts enumerated above, the son or sons of the dying man sit near his head and chant hymns from the *Vedas* to the dictation of the family priest. This is a most solemn occasion. The weeping and crying and other outward manifestations of mourning cease. The purport of the prayer is that all the sins of the dying man may be absolved and that he may find a happy abode in Heaven. When the dying man actually expires, the prayer ceases and all the relations go into the street mourning and wailing, facing the south—this amounts to an appeal to the God of Death—whose quarters are supposed to be in that direction—to show mercy to their dead relation. Then the whole household assembles round the dead person, and incessant weeping and wailing proceed for three or four hours. The males, however, do not give vent to their sorrow in this way, and generally keep themselves aloof. Some of the old-school women also come, having learned by heart several mourning ditties which they repeat, and make a pretence of weeping. If any of these old women have any insinuations to make, they take this opportunity of making them, and quarrels spring up—of course, after the mourning days are over. When the time for the removal of the corpse to the burning ground has arrived, the body has to be washed and decorated. The religious rites for the preparation of the sacred fire tc ignite the funeral pyre have to be performed near the corpse. The daughters and other close female relatives of the dead man bring water in pots and wash and decorate the body, while the sons perform the religious ceremony and prepare the sacred fire. In the meantime the construction of the bier goes on outside the house. When everything is ready, the leave-taking ceremony takes place. This consists in the dead man's palm being rubbed with as many two-anna pieces as there are close relatives, and these pieces being then presented to those relatives, who keep them as long as they live. When this is concluded, the corpse is placed on a bier of green palm leaves, the grandsons standing ready with lighted torches to accompany the bier to the burning ground. Young women stay at home but elderly ones always accompany the corpse. Arrived at the burning ground, elaborate religious ceremonies are gone through, at the end of each of which a large fee is paid to religious Brahmans, rich people sometimes spending a large sum of rupees on these funeral obsequies in the belief that any amount so expended always adds to the meritoriousness of the spender. After these rites the body is placed on the pyre and the fire lighted. The sons of the deceased sit down and are clean shaved, and after that bathe and return home with the other mourners. The sons and the wife of the dead man are the chief mourners. This almost ends the first day's rites.

On the second day, the rites commence very early in the morning. The funeral pyre is examined and the remains of the deceased are collected, while prayers are said and rites performed, milk and cocoanut water being sprinkled over the ashes to appease the thirst of the dead man's soul; and other oblations in the form of fried rice, pulses and dry cakes are offered. The funeral party then returns home. There a room is set apart, and in a corner of it a stone to represent the dead man's body is set up, and before noon every day certain rites are performed, which end in the offering of rice-balls to the soul of the dead man. These rice-balls are then carried out and thrown away in a pond or river. This mode of offering continues till the twelfth day, when the dead man is considered to have taken his place in Heaven along with the other departed relatives. This twelfth-day ceremony is called the *Sapindikarana*, meaning, adding the newly dead to those who have already departed, and not less than thirty-two donations, varying in value according to the pecuniary position of the parties, are offered. The first, second, tenth, eleventh and twelfth day ceremonies are the most sacred and tedious ones, but they are all gone through by the Hindus. The thirteenth day concludes the funeral rites, and is therefore called *Subhasvikarana*, meaning, resuming the usual mode of happy life after the mourning days are over. On this day the house is blessed by the priest, presents are given by the fathers-in-law to the sons who were engaged in these rites, and betel-leaf chewing, which was discontinued for the thirteen days, is resumed at night.

Let us now turn to the festive portion—if that term can be aptly applied to such a sorrowful occasion—of the funeral rites. The ancient Hindu sages have wisely ruled that certain close relatives should supply the mourning house with food on the mourning days. These relatives are the fathers or fathers-in-law (or the nearest male relatives in that direction) of the sons who perform the funeral rites. If the person who died has seven sons, the duty of supplying the mourning house with food falls on the fathers-in-law of all the seven sons, if they are all married, or, if not, on those of the sons who are married. The outside supply of food is necessary for the first, second, tenth, eleventh, twelfth and thirteenth days. If there are six different parties to undertake this kind of supply, they do it in turns. If their number is insufficient, some of these days are left out and only important days, as the first, tenth and the thirteenth, are chosen, or any one or two of these days. So far as the rule goes, it is a wise provision, for when the house goes into mourning, its comforts in the direction of feeding will be neglected unless some outside relation is chosen for the occasion. This duty of supply is called *sar vaikkiradu*, which means the supplying of food with pepper water ; only simple food is meant, and that was the rule in ancient days. But the modern Hindu custom is to supply a grand feast with all the modern art of which Hindu cookery is capable. All kinds of fruits, sweets and varieties of rice-preparations are offered to the mourners. One father-in-law vies with another in his competition to give grander and grander dinners on the successive days; and to crown the horror, quarrels sometimes spring up among some of these idiotic relations that due and proper invitation was not sent to such and such a party to be present at the dinner. Did the sages ever mean that their simple ruling should be thus abused by modern civilisation ? The sooner the old and orthodox custom is resumed the better. On the night of the thirteenth day presents in the shape of new cloths, rings and money are given to the boys and girls of the deceased by their relatives. A new cloth is worn by almost all and the mourning proper becomes a thing of the past. The monthly ceremonies are kept up and the annual ceremony closes the career of the dead man in his relationship with the world of the dead, and he becomes a *mane* or *pitri*.

8. Holi and Kamandi

IN the old days when demons were very powerful in India there was a she-demon named Holika. She was the most wicked of her race. Every day she would visit some town or village and carry away some of its children to feast upon them. These cruelties increased so much that the whole world complained to the king of the Rakshasas. Even that monarch who belonged to a proverbially cruel race was moved when he heard that all the children were being thus eaten up by Holika. He did not like to displease a female member of his own class. So he ordered that, as Holika had cultivated a special taste for children's flesh, the people should give her one child for her food every day, making their own arrangements to do so. Even this they considered a great favour and each house resolved to send by turn one child a day. When one village had thus had its turn, the next village or city, as the case may be, took up the arrangement. Thus several years passed. One day the lot fell upon a poor old woman and her grandson had to be sent up to Holika the next morning. That was her only child then—her son and her daughter-in-law having gone away long ago to the land from the borders of which no traveller returns. Her sorrow knew no bounds. She was soon to lose the last male member of her family. Her extreme sorrow moved the heart of every one, and Providence too seemed to pity her. It so happened that a holy mendicant chanced to pass by that village accidentally that day. He heard moanings in that old woman's house. He went to her and on making sympathetic enquiries learnt the cause. He was a holy person and after some contemplation found out the way by which he could save not only that old woman but the whole world from Holika's havocs. Said he:—"My good old woman! do not fear. Holika will die to-morrow if you only follow my advice. If she hears vile and indecent abuses and obscene expressions, she will fall down and die. It is so decreed. You should therefore collect all the children of the village and when Holika turns up to-morrow to demand your grandson, these children must severely rebuke her, using obscene and indecent expressions and making similar signs and symbols. She will pursue the children. They must not at all be afraid of her, but must continue to pour out vile abuses. And as it is so decreed, she must fall down dead." Having said this, the mendicant went away.

The old woman circulated the news in the village. As those days were days of strong beliefs, the villagers collected together all the boys and girls and backed them up secretly to attack Holika when pointed out. The plan worked excellently well and Holika died. The children joined together and cremated her body. This event is supposed to have happened on the full-moon day of the white-half of Phalguna, corresponding to the latter half of the month of March. And the Holi feast of the Hindus originates from this legend.

In Madras the Mahrattas and Lalas—mostly non-Brahmans—observe this feast with all sorts of hideousness. The Brahmans—Mahrattas—celebrate it by a feast. In other parts of India all castes more or less observe the Holi. There is no religious ceremony of any kind connected with this, but there is more than any reasonable amount of foolish practices associated with it. During the observance of this feast the youngsters of the Lala sect in Madras make, in each house or in common for a whole street, an image of Holika, sing obscene songs before it, offer sweetmeats, fruits and other things in mock-worship of the image, exchange horse-play compliments by syringing coloured-water on each other's clothes and spend the whole period of the feast like merry butterflies singing and chatting and abusing. Indecent language is allowed to be indulged in during the continuance of this jolly occasion. At about 1 A.M., on the full-moon day, the image of Holika is burnt, and children sit round the embers and beat their mouths making a mock-mourning sound. Tender children are shown over the fire for a second by the fond mothers and this process is believed to remove all kinds of danger from the babies.

Such is the origin of this feast, which, however, very few happen to know. Most of the observers of this feast imagine that the object they worship is Cupid and that the mock-funs they observe are on account of Kama, the God of Love. And this feast which is observed as the Holi in Madras and Northern India is known as Kaman-pandikai in the South. And the images of Cupid and his wife Rati are painted, worshipped and burnt on the same day and hour as the image of Holika. And it is also most curious to see that this Kaman-pandikai in the South is observed more by the adults than by the children who also take part in it. The burning of Cupid by Siva has been sung by more than one Hindu poet; but none has done it so beautifully as Kalidasa in his *Kumarasambhava*, or the "Birth of the War-god." The story briefly runs thus: There was a mighty Titan in times of yore named Tarakasura. He was such a great terror to the celestials and *a fortiori* to the mortals. One day he is said to have invaded the Divine world and carried away all the damsels from Indra's harem. The sun-god by his order shone like the moon. The wind-god was by a similar command wafting soft and sweet breeze ever by the side of this Titan. The celestials were terrified at his havocs. The Divine assembly met to concert measures to put down Taraka. Brihaspati, Indra's minister, rose up and said that the offspring of Siva and Parvati—Kumara—can destroy that powerful Titan. But Siva was a sage who was performing penance. How to make him court Parvati? The council sent for Cupid and he boastingly appeared before the lord of the celestials and said that he would bind any being, whether God or man, by the chain of woman's love. Indra was greatly pleased. It was just what he wanted. So he sent Cupid to Siva, requesting him to dart his arrows rather cautiously, as Siva was no ordinary God. And Cupid too, when he was told the name of the deity that he had to conquer by his arrows, became terrified. He was unable to withdraw. So he went to the hermitage of Siva. At Cupid's approach, the birds and beasts of the forest danced with joy at the sudden setting-in of the Spring season. The drone drank the honey which remained after the bee had first drunk to her fill. Parvati was helping Siva with flowers, fruits and other things which were required for that god's penance. Cupid considered that everything was extremely favourable to him. He fixed the arrow of love to his bow and was taking his aim at Siva. The ever-holy mind of Siva wavered a bit and he cast his looks on Parvati, who appeared all the more beautiful that day decorated from top to toe with all the flowers that Spring had brought into existence in that hermitage. Then Siva suddenly regaining his balance of mind, laughed at his own weakness and looked round to see the cause of it. He saw Cupid at a distance. The celestials who were watching from above noticed the rage of Siva. "Please subdue your anger and save poor Cupid," begged they. But before that noise reached the ears of Siva, a small spark of fire got unloosened from the third eye in his forehead and left Cupid an image of ashes. This event is believed to have occurred on the full-moon day of Phalguna. It is the death of Cupid in this unhappy manner that is celebrated as Kaman-pandikai in South India. A flag called the flag of Cupid is left planted for four or five days before the full-moon day, in a prominent place in every street, is worshipped with love songs and other frolics and is burnt on the full-moon day.

As both these events, the death of Holika and the death of Cupid, occurred on the same day, this feast is called the *Holi* feast by some and as *Kaman-pandikai* by others, the first five days' feast before the full-moon being called the *Holi-pandikai* and the next three days as the *Kaman-pandikai*. As the *Holi* feast is celebrated to remove the evils of youngsters and children, *Kaman-pandikai* is supposed to be observed to remove the evils that may accrue to adults and grown-up men by the setting-in of the Spring. If they go wrong their body will be reduced to ash as was Cupid's, is the moral.

9. Kalakshepas—Old and New

ONE of the striking ways in which Hindu Revivalism has made itself particularly visible, specially among the Hindu community in Madras, in recent years, is the weekly gatherings in different parts of the city to hear religious discourses by professional preachers. These discourses are known as *Kalakshepas* in the sacred language of the East. What is a *Kalakshepa?* The word is a Sanskrit compound formed of two simple words meaning "the whiling away of time." The history of the word can be traced to the early days of the earliest of the *Puranas*.

In the good old times of Ancient India, whenever a king or any great personage celebrated a religious sacrifice, several learned persons from remote parts of the country came, on invitation, to take part in the celebration, their primary duty being to assist in the religious rites. And these rites extended over a large space of time, in some instances to as many as twelve years and in some to as few as twelve days. But the generality of sacred rites lasted for a period of twelve months; and the spots chosen for such celebrations were the banks of a stream or river with beautiful groves or other natural scenery. The ceremonies connected with the performance of the rites were invariably gone through in the first half of the day, and the royal host had to provide some sort of diversion for the guests for the other half. And this diversion had, from early times, been called *Kalakshepa*. The guests, among whom were hundreds of men learned in various branches of study, often had new and old ideas to communicate to and exchange with each other. The sages of old utilised the occasion of such unique gatherings not merely for the pleasant whiling away of their time but more particularly for the instruction and mutual enlightenment of the guests. After the midday meal, these learned men assembled under the cool and refreshing shades of the spacious trees of the hermitage and spent their time in the most pleasant and useful manner possible. A few who were learned in philosophy would form themselves into a group under a stately banyan and discuss the several systems of their special branch of study. Another group under the sacred pipal, probably codifiers like Manu, would discuss the revisions and emendations of moral and ethical codes. A third batch would be clearing their doubts regarding their intonation in the chanting of Vedic hymns. Thus according to their tastes and inclinations the learned sages grouped themselves into batches and carried on discussions in their lines of thought; and at the end of the period of the sacrifice they left the hermitage not only enriched by the liberal gifts of the host but with increased knowledge acquired from exchange of thoughts with their fellow professors, which knowledge they diffused among the people at large during their travels from place to place.

Such gatherings, which in the old days may be said to have somewhat corresponded to the present day *British Association* stripped of all its modern environments, were the result of the ancient form of *Kalakshepa*. And students of oriental literature will find descriptions of such gatherings in the pages of the ancient epics of India, such as the *Mahabharata* and the *Ramayana*. Nay, the whole of the *Mahabharata* is said to have been related during one of these long sacrifices. In ancient times *Kalakshepas* were few and far between. But wherever and whenever such took place they always resulted in a substantial addition to the literature of the country and the enlightenment of the people at large.

But now these *Kalakshepas* have multiplied like mushrooms and in many cases persons with no pretensions to learning stand up as preachers. The original object of instruction is lost sight of, and Mammon is the God presiding over most of these exhibitions. Most of the *Bhagavatas* are self-styled; and having managed to get a smattering knowledge of a few puranic tales, they make *Kalakshepa* of these tales, not on religious occasions but invariably during the *Rahukala* time of a Sunday evening, nor before learned assemblies always, as in days of old, but often before unlearned and uncritical audiences. In the majority of instances at the present day it is the inspiring nature of the themes chosen for *Kalakshepa* and the accompaniment of music that attract large crowds to such discourses more than the learning or powers of exposition of the preacher. Whether the audiences return home the wiser for having attended such lectures or not, there can be no doubt that the *Bhagavatas* return the richer; for, their fees, in most cases, for a lecture range from Rs. 10 to 100 according to their power to amuse, instruct or divert the audience. One with a decidedly musical talent is more popular among the people than one with mere learning. Sometimes these modern *Bhagavatas* drive in coaches to their places of preaching while the sages of the old had perhaps to perform their long and tedious journeys on foot. Some of them robe themselves in silks and shawls and glitter in diamonds, while the *Bhagavatas* of old were content perhaps with the bark of trees. Many of the popular *Bhagavatas* often earn Rs. 200 to 500 and sometimes more a month. For all that what is an average *Bhagavata?* When compared with the sages of old most of the modern *Bhagavatas* have only a show of knowledge and are yet admired by an audience who wonder "how such a small head could carry so much wonderful knowledge" in Tamil, Telugu, Kanarese, Sanskrit, Mahratti, Hindustani, and sometimes English also. As is the *Bhagavata*, so is the audience.

But in these days of widespread irreverence and irreligion, preachers, however poor in attainments and however low they have fallen from the standard of the ideal preachers of old, still have some power of God in their hands, provided the Hindu public who are catered for by these professionals learn to be discriminating in the bestowal of their patronage and exacting in their judgment of the qualifications and capabilities of the preachers. There are many religious organizations in Madras, which ought to combine for their common good and resolve to encourage only the really learned among these professionals. A great responsibility therefore lies on the leaders of the Hindu community in this matter, and, if only they introduce wholesome reforms in their field of popular education a great deal of good might in time be expected by the people.

10. The Mukkoti or Vaikuntha Ekadasi

THE word *Ekadasi* means the eleventh day of a fortnight, and there are thus two *Ekadasis* every month. All the twenty-four *Ekadasis* throughout the year are sacred to a Hindu. Strict fasting and prayer have to be observed throughout the *Ekadasi* day. The orthodox Hindu bathes early in the morning in a running stream, tank, or well, and goes through a series of prayers. ' He must not hold any conversation with persons of low caste, with those who have renounced the Hindu religion, with liars, with thieves and others of abandoned character. The company of those who are in the habit of plundering the property of others or temple property must be strictly avoided on the *Ekadasi* day. The orthodox Hindu observing this fast must raise his eyes towards the sun to expiate the sin of having seen these bad people, if ever he happens to meet them on this day. He should spend his whole time in worshipping Govinda by flowers, fruits, incense and Vedic hymns.

He must avoid bad or cruel words in talking to people. He must fast day and night and devote his whole time to pure religious thoughts and prayers—all of which must relate only to the god Krishna. *Ekadasi* of the dark half of the month is as pure as that of the light half of the month. He who observes the *Ekadasi* strictly gets all the meritoriousness that is ascribed to the performance of charitable acts during the solar or lunar eclipses or to the performance of the *Asvamedha* or horse-sacrifice. The meritoriousness which is attained by an anchorite after performing penance for full sixty thousand years is acquired by him who observes but one *Ekadasi*-fast rigidly. The fame which is attained by a donation of 1,000 cows to Brahmans is acquired by him who observes a single *Ekadasi* correctly. The keeping of this fast is more meritorious than the giving of acres as gifts to Brahmans, and more holy than imparting the sacred knowledge of the *Vedas* to students. It is several times superior to feeding starving men, for it is the day most sacred to Vishnu. The observance of this fast on this day gives one eternal felicity in the heavens. The pilgrimage to the holy waters and sacred places is recommended only to those who have not understood the sanctity of the *Ekadasi*. All the hard penances of a rigid anchorite are prompted by utter stupidity inasmuch as he could easily avoid them if he would observe but one *Ekadasi* strictly. He who observes the *Ekadasi* attains all his ends and he who does not observe it is the worst of sinners.'

This is the description given in the *Bhavishyottara-purana* of the sanctity of the *Ekadasi*. Every orthodox Hindu, be he Smarta, Vaishnava or Madhva, has to observe this fast rigidly. Some of the Vaishnavas and the Madhvas have such a great regard for the *Ekadasi* fasting that they give up on this day the performance of the annual ceremonies to satisfy the manes of their departed forefathers if the ceremonies happen to fall on this day. The Smartas and some of the Vaishnavas will consider this as amounting to giving up the ceremonies, inasmuch as they are not performed on the day on which they fall. But those Vaishnavas and the Madhvas who give up the ceremonies have their own arguments for doing so. When they do not themselves eat on the *Ekadasi* day, the manes of their forefathers have no claim to be fed by ceremonies and so the right to perform these ceremonies rises only on the day succeeding the fasting day. The observance of the *Ekadasi* day is not solely based upon puranic belief. There are several *Upanishads*, which are regarded to be equal in sacredness to the *Vedas* and which also attribute the greatest sanctity to the observance of the *Ekadasi* fast.

All this is about *Ekadasi* in general. And it must once for all be said that an orthodox Hindu looks upon all the *Ekadasis* at all times of the year as the same, as far as their sanctity is concerned. He does not attribute more sacredness to one and less to another. But by the Vaishnavas, the *Mukkoti* or *Vaikuntha Ekadasi* is considered the most holy of all the *Ekadasis*. No direct authority for this belief so far as we know exists anywhere in the sacred writings of the Hindus. The *Purānas* and the *Upanishads* speak of the sacredness of *Ekadasi* in general and on this head all are agreed. But what is the reason for attributing special sanctity to the

Mukkoti Ekadasi which occurs in December—January? The following seems to be the explanation:—Krishna in the *Bhagavadgita* says to Arjuna that if he—the deity—is looked at in the light of months, he is the month of *Margasira* (12th December—11th January). The idea is that this month is more to the liking of the God. As the *Mukkoti Ekadasi* falls in the light half of this month it must have been held specially sacred by the Brahmans. This sacred day of the light fortnight of *Margasira*, this *Mukkoti Ekadasi*, is represented as a female deity in the *Brahmanda-purana* (the gender of *Ekadasi* is feminine) and to have originated from the body of Krishna himself. The statement of Krishna in the *Gita* that he is the month of *Margasira* among months and the story in the *Brahmandapurana* that the goddess presiding over this *Ekadasi* sprung from the body of Krishna himself must be the main reasons for the *Mukkoti Ekadasi* being held highly sacred by the Hindus. Apart from both these, there is another cause why the Vaishnavas deem this day most sacred. One of their great sages, Nammalwar attained his felicity—*Vaikuntha*—on this day, according to

Vaishnava legends. The thirty-three crores of gods are said to have come down to witness it. Hence this *Ekadasi* is called *Vaikuṇtha Ekadasi* or *Mukkoti Ekadasi*, which latter is a shortened form of *Muppattu Mukkoti Ekadasi*.

In Vishnu temples a special gateway leading to the shrine is opened on this day and he who passes through this doorway is considered to have passed through the gates of *Vaikuntha* or the abode of felicity in the heavens, like Nammalwar, a famous Vaishnava saint. The Madhvas and the Smartas who observe the *Ekadasi* equally well with the Vaishnavas do not appear to attach any special merit for the passage through this special gateway, which is called the *Vaikuntha* gateway.

The *Mukkoti Ekadasi* is observed in all Vaishnava temples. Ten days before and ten days after it are also held sacred by the Vaishnava sect of the Tenkalai class, as the recitation of *Tiruvaymoli*—the Tamil *Vaishnava Veda*—is supposed to have taken place before the god Ranganatha in Srirangam on these days. In this sacred island-shrine of the Vaishnavas this feast is celebrated in grand style and pilgrims flock to it from all parts of India.

11. The Krittika

THE *Krittika* is a feast in honour of the glory of Siva. The legend regarding this feast is as follows: Brahma and Vishnu had a dispute among themselves as to who was the superior of the two, and appealed to Siva. To decide the superiority, Siva devised a means. He said that he would stand up as an all-pervading pillar of fire, that Brahma should traverse the sky and discover the top of the pillar, and that Vishnu should find his way to the nether world and discover the foot of it. Brahma called at once his swan vehicle and started, and Vishnu assumed the form of a boar and went on boring and boring to the nether world and down and down to discover the foot. He, who returned first and reported what he was asked to see, was to be pronounced the superior of the two. That was the test of superiority. So Brahma and Vishnu were very busy travelling one to the upper and the other to the nether world. They are said to have gone on and on and on for several *Yugas* (eras) with no avail. While Brahma was travelling up he observed a *Ketaki* (Tamil: *Talambu*) flower, the sweet scented flower of the screwpine, travelling down towards the earth. It is stated that Brahma stopped the flower and asked him to relate his history. "O, I was on the head of Siva several centuries ago. I left it and am going down to the earth. O, what a long travel I have had! How far is the earth yet from this place? And who are you, please, and what is your object in travelling up," said the flower. Brahma:—"I am Brahma, and was asked by Siva to discover the top of his head. I left the earth several *Yugas* ago. If what you say is true, I have not done half the way yet. But will you mind doing me a small favour? Vishnu and I were asked by Siva to discover his head and foot, respectively. I shall say that I saw the head, and cite you as my witness. You must confirm me as you say that you occupied once that part of Siva's body" "Agreed," said the screwpine flower, for, as he had a long journey to perform to reach the earth, he liked the idea of securing a companion in Brahma for his travels and this he could gain by uttering a petty lie. So Brahma and the *Ketaki* flower started together on their downward journey and came to Siva after several *Yugas*. Brahma, of course, had carefully got by heart what he had heard from the *Ketaki* about the head of Siva. As soon as they reached the earth, Brahma said to Siva :—"Holy Sir ! I have seen your head." Siva understood in himself by his superior powers that it was impossible. Still, to prove that Brahma was uttering a lie, he asked him to describe it. Brahma repeated the story that he had heard from the flower and cited the *Ketaki* as his witness. "Vile wretch," said Siva to the screwpine, "as you have uttered a falsehood before me, may you never be used in my worship." And even to this day the sweet scented screwpine flower, on account of this curse of Siva, is never used in Siva temples for the worship of Siva. And as Brahma lied before Siva he was cursed to go without temples in this earth. So even now Brahma has no temple in the whole of India. Thus in short runs the legend.

The Krittika feast is celebrated to commemorate the occasion of Siva's having stood up as a fire-pillar on this day. What the Dipavali is to the Gujaratis in the Gujaratipet of Madras, so is Krittika to the other Hindus. A row of lights will be observed in front of every house on this night in the whole of Southern India. Children take to firing crackers. The non-Brahman population of Madras wear new cloths on this day. As Siva is supposed to have appeared in the form of a pillar of radiance on this day, in every place where there is a Siva temple a big rod some 25 or 30 feet high is planted opposite to the temple in an open space and left covered up with a thick coating of dried palm leaves from top to bottom. The whole work assumes the form of a leafy cylinder of about five feet in diameter. In the evening, after sun-set, the Siva god of the village or town is taken out of the temple in procession. The procession stops before the cylinder. A brief ceremonial worship is performed and then lighted camphor is thrown at the foot of the cylinder. The whole work now blazes up and a great conflagration ensues which, of course, is so well arranged as not to injure any house or property. While this cylinder continues to burn, the worshippers assembled there throw pulverised resin over it. This is the closing of the feast in temples situated in the plains. As soon as the leafy pillar is reduced to ashes, the villagers assembled collect the embers which are considered to be the body of Siva, and miraculous powers are attributed to them. Sometimes they are used for manuring the fields in the expectation of a good harvest. In the places sacred to Siva, where temples are situated on the tops of mountains, the burning of the leafy pillar takes place a day after that observed in the plains. Sometimes a big caldron containing ghee, camphor and other combustibles is lighted on the mountain top and this continues to burn for a whole month. At Tiruvannamalai, Trichinopoly, Tiruttani, Mayilam, and other places where the temples are situated on hills, the whole rock on which the pagoda stands is illuminated and the sight is rendered as grand as temple funds will admit. The view at Tiruvannamalai on the Krittika feast night is supposed to be the grandest in Southern India. This feast takes place in the month of Krittika (November—December) when the constellation of that name is in conjunction with the moon, which occurs on the full-moon day of this month. What Shah-e-berat is to Muhammadans so is Krittika to the Hindus—a night of illuminations and lights. This feast is generally supposed to conclude a course of heavy rains that follow the North-East Monsoon. "After Krittika there is no rain" is the Tamil proverb —"*Karttikaikkappuram malai illai.*" As in the Dipavali, there are special presents in the Krittika feast also to the newly married bride in the shape of cloths, vessels, brass or bronze lamps, and others.

12. The Mahamakha

THE full-moon day of the month of Kumbha (corresponding to 12th February to 12th March) is held sacred by the Hindus throughout India for bathing in the sacred tank called the Mahamakha-saras in Kumbakonam. This occasion, which occurs annually, is called the *Makham*, *i.e.*, the occasion when the moon passes through the asterism of *Makham* in the month of *Kumbha*. But the *Mahamakham* or the great *Makham* is an event which occurs only once in twelve years. The planet Jupiter takes twelve years to complete one revolution round the sun and during this course when it is in conjunction with the moon in the *Makha* asterism of the constellation of Leo—*Simha*—the *Mahamakham* occurs. This is an astronomical incident which takes place only once in twelve years, and when it takes place the event is celebrated as above mentioned. All the holy rivers and bathing places on the seashore are resorted to on this occasion; but the Hindu who takes his bath in the holy waters of the *Mahamakham* tank at Kumbakonam is considered to have reaped the beneficial effects of several baths in all the holy waters of India. Such being the belief of the Hindus an account of the origin of the *Mahamakham* festival may be interesting. The *Mahamakham* tank, which is the biggest one in Kumbakonam, is situated in the south-eastern portion of the town and is about a mile to the west of the South Indian Railway Station there. In shape it is a nine-sided polygon with five re-entrant angles. Two very old Siva temples dedicated to Abhimukteswara and Visvanatha are situated respectively on its eastern and northern sides, and streets run on the other two sides. The legend of the tank, as disclosed by the *Sthalapurana* of Kumbakonam, runs as follows:—Under the orders of Siva, Brahma collected the essence of all the sacred waters in the world in a pot and mixed with it the nectar (*devamrita*) also. He most carefully secured this pot on the top of the mountain Meru. But during the great deluge, when the world was destroyed by an overflowing inundation, the pot somehow lost its position and was observed floating on the water. At the end of the deluge, when the waters subsided, the pot rested in a place now called Kumbakonam and at the spot where the temple of Kumbheswara—from whom the town derives its name—is situated. The compound word "Kumbakonam," which is the name of the city, comes from two simple Sanskrit words *kumbha* meaning an earthen pot and *ghona* the nostril or neck of it. Thus the name of the city is connected with the pot of Brahma. But to continue the legend :—When at the beginning of the creation of the world after the deluge, the god Siva was wandering over the earth in the disguise of a hunter, he saw this earthen pot, and as he then held a bow in his hand, he aimed, in sportive mood, at the neck of the pot. The pot broke and the holy water in it began to flow out. It found its level in a hollow pit. This is the very same pit that has become now, according to the legend, the sacred tank of *Mahamakhasaras* at Kumbakonam. When Siva saw the pot break, he made a *lingam* out of sand and placed it over the pot and infused his own fiery energy into it. When this was done, Brahma came down from the upper regions with thirty-three crores of *devas* and worshipped the *lingam* in befitting style. He was engaged in his prayers for a very long time, and came to the close on a *Mahamakham* day. He got up from his contemplative position and proceeded to bathe in the tank before him. But lo! a most holy congregation was before him. The great gods Nageswara, Mukteswara and others, the goddesses of all the holy waters of the world—Ganga, Yamuna, Setu, etc., were already waiting there to bathe in the tank along with the lord of creation—Brahma. Even the deity of Benares—Visveswara—had come there not to lose the rare opportunity. They all greeted Brahma and praised him for his faith in Siva. Brahma proceeded to bathe in the tank by way of bringing the period of his contemplation to a close, and all the gods followed suit and took their baths. These events occurred on a *Mahamakham* day, and from that time forward bathing in this tank on the *Mahamakham* occasion has come to be considered as equal to bathing in all the sacred rivers and before all the gods. Such then is, according to the legend, the origin of this tank and of this festival.

Every orthodox Hindu believes that the holy waters of the Ganges come down to this tank on this occasion. Most of the old Brahmans will say that they observed the goddess Ganga raise one of her hands from underneath the surface of the water of this sacred tank to announce to the anxious pilgrims her arrival in the tank, and that soon after, a lime fruit, a garland of flowers and a roll of palm leaf were seen floating on the water. The latter are considered to be the signs of the visit of a deity, especially of a female deity. The preliminaries to this festival commence ten days before the *Mahamakham* day. From distant quarters of India pilgrims flock to Kumbakonam in very large numbers. On the *Mahamakham* day all the principal idols of Siva in the town march in procession to this tank. Thousands of pilgrims and devotees follow these idols chanting hymns in praise of the holy rivers. When the procession reaches the pillar post near the Nageswara temple one great mass of moving heads is observed from that elevated position as far as the eyes can reach to the East, South, North and West. For, *Mahamakham* is considered the greatest occasion in India, and large crowds flock to witness it. The municipal authorities take the precaution of reducing the depth of the water in the tank and leave only water just sufficient to enable the pilgrims to bathe without danger of being drowned. This wise precaution has been taken from time immemorial; but instead of the steam engines now used, piccotahs or country water-lifts were used in those old days. The idols of gods that march in procession are temporarily accommodated in the *mandapams* on the banks of the tank. The trident which is the emblem of Siva is taken out by the priest of each god and immersed in water. This is the signal that that particular god to whom the trident belongs has himself performed the bathing ceremony in the tank This is also the signal that the holy occasion for the bathing of the people has set in. The twelve tridents are immersed simultaneously in twelve different spots of the tank, and along with these, thousands of devotees plunge their heads into the waters with the firm belief that they are bathing in the quintessence of all the sacred rivers, and in the presence of all the gods. Every one gets up from the bath with his whole body besmeared with mud, but for all that, he goes home with the consolation that the holy occasion has been availed of and that the holy bathing in all the sacred rivers has been taken in one plunge. Such is faith, simple faith, more consoling than all philosophy. What Jerusalem is to the Christians, what Buddha-Gaya is to the Buddhists, what Mecca is to the Muhammadans, what Benares is to the Indian—so is the *Mahamakham* bath to all the Hindus on the *Mahamakham* day. As the water in this tank is supposed to have originated first from the earthen pot so carefully guarded by Brahma, this tank goes also by the name of *Brahma-tirtham*. Owing to the special sanctity attached to it on this occasion, the tank is also called the *Mahamakhasaras*. It is also called *Kanyatirtham* after the goddesses *Kanyas* on the tank. These *kanyas* or virgins are supposed to be the representations of nine holy waters :—*Ganga*, *Yamuna*, *Narmada*, *Sarasvati*, *Godavari*, *Krishna*, *Kaveri*, *Tambraparni*, and *Kanyakumari*.

The bath in the *Mahamakham* tank on this sacred occasion is considered to wipe off all sins. The river Ganges is supposed to run into the *Mahamakham* tank by a subterranean current, *Antarvahini*, on this day and the Hindu devotee will assert that if on this sacred occasion the water in the Ganges is examined it will be noticed to have gone down by one foot. Where did the waters go! Of course to the *Mahamakham* tank! How did they go? By the—*Antarvahini*—under current. In connection with this strong belief the following story is related:—

In the good old days, before the Kaliyuga had set in, there was a very pious king reigning over the country of Mithila, north of Benares. He was happy in every way except that he had not a son to succeed to his throne. Once upon a time a holy sage, a *rishi*, visited the king and told him that if he bathed in the waters of the sacred Ganges on the *Mahamakham* day he would soon obtain a son. The king had the greatest respect for the sage and desired to follow his advice. He proclaimed his intention among his subjects, and several of these, who were unhappy like the king in not having sons, followed their sovereign. Each started with his wife also; for the Hindu belief is that bathing in holy waters is not complete unless both the husband and the wife hold each the other's hand and bathe together in the waters facing the current. So on that *Mahamakham* day before the Kali-yuga several thousands of families bathed thus in the Ganges with the king of Mithila. All got out of the water safe, except the king and his queen. What became of the royal pair, no one knew. A very careful search was made. The river was dragged with nets. Not the slightest clue could be had. It was a perfect mystery to every one. The loyal subjects returned to their homes with dismal faces and regarded the event as a great calamity.

But the fact was that the king with his queen got out safe from his bathing. But instead of meeting with their own people, he and his wife found themselves in the middle of a strange tank, and in the middle of people speaking strange tongues. For the royal pair got out of their bathing at Kumbakonam and not at Benares where they plunged themselves in the Ganges, because the subterranean current of the Ganges had carried the pair to the *Mahamakham* tank at Kumbakonam. The royal pair had travelled the long distance in the twinkling of an eye. With difficulty they explained themselves to the people at Kumbakonam and found out the real state of affairs. The king's desire has already been fulfilled; for he had a boy. Such is the story and it is very interesting as it is proof positive to the pious devotee that subterranean communication between the Ganges and the *Mahamakham* tank exists even to-day.

The sacredness of grand rivers generally is a strong Hindu belief and the special sanctity attributed to certain waters on an occasion occurring only once in twelve years is equally a strong Hindu belief. *Pushkaram* is the *Mahamakham* of the Telugus, and occurs only once in twelve years, when the freshes of the Godavari rise to a very high level. Bathing on the *Pushkaram* day at certain chosen spots on the banks of the Godavari is considered as sacred by the Telugus as the *Mahamakham* bath is by all Hindus.

13. The Arddhodaya and the Mahodaya

THE Hindus regard the two occasions of *Arddhodaya* and *Mahodaya* as very sacred occasions for taking baths in holy rivers and in sacred spots on the seashore. The *Arddhodaya* is considered to be the more sacred of the two. It is the rising of the sun and the moon in conjunction at the beginning of which the sun is in Capricorn—*Makara*—on a Sunday in the month of *Pushya* (January-February) and the moon in the 22nd asterism—*Sravana* and the seventh *Yoga*. These five events do not occur in conjunction oftener than once in sixty years. The most important circumstance in the *Arddhodaya* is the half-rising of the sun with which are connected the four events above mentioned. Owing to this half-rising of the sun this occasion is called the *Arddhodaya*, which is a Sanskrit compound meaning the half-rising. Thus the *Arddhodaya* is a very rare opportunity for sacred baths and we have no recollection of its occurrence in the immediate past.

But the *Mahodaya* occurs oftener. It is considered a little less meritorious as compared with the *Arddhodaya*, but for all that it is also considered a very sacred opportunity for baths. The *Mahodaya* is the rising of the sun and the moon in conjunction on a Monday, the sun being in Capricorn, in the month of *Pushya* (January-February) and the moon in the asterism of *Sravana* when it is in conjunction with *Vyatipata yoga*. The last *Mahodayas* occurred on Monday, the 5th February, 1894, and on the 1st February, 1895. Both the *Arddhodaya* and the *Mahodaya* are deemed to be very sacred occasions for religious bathing, alms-giving, propitiating the spirits of the departed forefathers, and performing other religious duties. Wealthy Hindus generally go on pilgrimages to Benares and Rameswaram to bathe in the sacred waters in these places. The sacred water of *Dhanushkoti* near Rameswaram is considered to be most holy on this occasion as it is said to have been opened by Rama with his bow. The Hindus of Madras generally proceed to Mahabalipuram—the

Seven Pagodas—to bathe in the sea on this occasion.

MAHODAYAM AT MAHABALIPUR

The small village of Mahabalipuram assumes an unusually busy appearance at the *Mahodayam*, a special New Moon day occurring on a Monday in the month of *Pushya*. This special New Moon day occurs once in 30 years and as such is considered extremely sacred by the Hindus. Pilgrimages are undertaken to Benares and Rameswaram for baths in the holy Ganges or in the *Dhanushkoti*. Orthodox Hindus who have not the time and convenience for such undertakings, go to some sacred place situated on the sea: and Mahabalipuram on the Madras Coast is a specially sacred place for occasions like this. From the Sunday previous country carts begin to pour in from all directions notwithstanding the difficulties of the marshes on all the sides of this little village. More than a thousand carts could be seen in this place, and boats from the Adyar would be emptying pilgrim-passengers here in several hundreds every hour. The petty traders of Madras make a good profit in selling fruits and other petty things. On the morning of the Monday, more than fifteen thousand heads are seen bathing in the sea. The whole shore would be one mass of Hindus and most fortunately there are generally no accidents of any kind. Mahabalipuram is known to the European world by the antiquarian remains in which this village is rich and which have been well described to the public by many eminent writers on antiquities. All the pilgrim sojourners visit these remains after the bath and the ideas they express of what they see are very amusing and give us an insight into their knowledge of their own history. "These are the caves where the Pandavas lived," say some. "No," denies another with all the authority of a historian and states that these caves were constructed by Rishis. A third greyhead, with anger in his face, states that Mahabali was a very powerful sovereign, that even gods from the heavens were visiting him every day, and it was to accommodate them that Mahabali built these caves. These and such like are the theories. But not one is to be seen expressing a wish to know anything historically about these relics. No one studies or attempts to study them, though several works exist already giving as much as inquiry has hitherto been able to ascertain of information on this subject. Whether these caves accommodated the gods at the time of Mahabali or not, it cannot be denied that they now accommodate the pilgrim-sojourners of Mahabalipuram. Thousands and thousands of people find their home now in these Pallava caves. This village is very small and house accommodation is very scanty, the number of ruined houses and those now in occupation being not more than eighty. And where could the fifteen thousand pilgrims find their home for a day now but in these caves? The whole place is full of people, the major portion being Vaishnavas, by which sect this place is held specially sacred. The bath and sight-seeing of the relics are generally over by about 10 in the morning and the pilgrims return home for breakfast. Fortunately a good supply of provisions is kept ready by the merchants. But the supply of pure water is not sufficient, and this difficulty is not felt as the sojourners are all to return to their respective homes by the evening. Visitors from Madras generally go down to Mahabalipuram by the Canal and return by the land route *via* Tirukkalukkunram and Chingleput. There is no road between Mahabalipuram and Tirukkalukkunram. There is a rough path by the thick copse of shrub wood in which the whole plain round about Mahabalipuram abounds, and a walk through it by the setting sun repays all the pain and trouble of a day's sojourn at Mahabalipuram. The fine breeze, the rosy rays of the setting sun, the scenery of the blue flowers of the *Kasan* shrub, the fluttering peacock which happens to be peculiar to this copse, and the sweet scent of a thousand wild flowers cheer the exhausted pilgrim and when the sun sets, the heart of the pilgrim droops down with the approaching night. To add to his gloom the copse changes into marsh and broken country tracks with ruts and muddy pools—till Tirukkalukkunram is reached. Thence it is all a nice road to Chingleput, which is performed in two hours by a jutka.

14. The Sarasvati Puja

SARASVATI in Hindu Mythology is the goddess of speech and learning and represented as the wife of Brahma, the creator or the supreme spirit. The ninth day of the month of Avani, corresponding to October, is considered most sacred in the year to this goddess. Generally the first nine days—*Navaratri*—of the bright half of this month is considered sacred either to Durga, Lakshmi, or Sarasvati, and throughout India worship on a grand scale is performed to these goddesses. Though these days are thus sacred to one goddess or other, the last 3 days, from the 7th to the 9th of the *Navaratri*, are specially sacred to the goddess of learning, and the last of these festive days, the *Navami*, closes the ceremony by the worship of Sarasvati. During the *Navaratri* days all the toys available in a Hindu household are displayed in fanciful arrangements in a large hall with the goddess Durga, Lakshmi, or Sarasvati in the middle, and this display is supposed to represent the penance of these goddesses. The Madhvas and the Vaishnavas would call this the penance of Lakshmi, and would point out to the grand feast at Tirupati during this period as their authority. In the Tirupati hills there is a Brahmotsavam held during this period representing the penance of Lakshmi and the festival closes on this day with Lakshmi's wedding to Vishnu. The Sivites term this *Durgapuja*, and this name appears to be more correct, as the greatest portion of India regards the *Navaratri* as sacred to Durga. Durga's hard penance to secure Siva, as her lord is known to every Hindu and is sung by the best of their poets; so that it does not require any special mention here. The Advaitis, in keeping with their school, worship all the three goddesses, on this occasion and commence their *puja* with salutation to Durga, Lakshmi and Sarasvati.

We have already alluded to the display of toys in every Hindu household. Women and children take great pleasure in collecting during this occasion as many toys as possible.

Every evening during these nine days, they spend an hour or two in singing the praises of these goddesses, and after this is over, distribute *pan supari* and sweets. This ceremony is confined only to women and children; male members do not take part in it. It is near this display of toys—the *kolu*, as it is called in the south of India—that all the available books of a Hindu household are arranged for the day and there the goddess Sarasvati is worshipped. A silver, copper or brass *chombu* filled with rice to the brim, with a cocoanut over it, serves to represent any goddess. Sometimes a gold jewel serves as an ornament to this vessel. Just at midday the head of the family takes his seat in the middle of the hall to perform the *puja* and all the children assemble round him. Strict fasting is observed till the worship is over. Young boys, though their mothers may permit them to eat their food, will not touch anything lest the goddess Sarasvati be displeased. When the head of the house finishes his *puja* all the others assembled there stand up with flowers in their hands reciting the praises of Sarasvati to the dictation of the master and offer the same to the goddess. Thus concludes the *Sarasvati puja* and a sumptuous feast in honour of the goddess follows. People who are rich present clothes on this occasion to married women. The origin of this ceremony is to be found in the *Skanda Purana.* It runs briefly as follows :—

In the Kritayuga there lived a famous King named Suketu. He was well versed in politics and his only pleasure was to attend to the welfare and comfort of his subjects. The name of his queen was Suvedi. She was young, beautiful and much attached to her lord. It so happened that Suketu was defeated by his enemies and compelled to fly for his life with his queen. The royal pair wandered in a forest for several days without food and, unable to bear the exhaustion, fell ill. Suvedi carried her weak lord on her shoulders and was trying to find her way out of the woods when she was met by the sage Angiras who said: "Who are you that have ventured alone into this deep forest? You seem to be much afflicted. Relate your history and I shall try my best to relieve you." Suvedi related her history and Angiras was extremely moved on hearing it. The sage at once recommended to Suvedi, a pilgrimage to Panchavati and the worship of Durga there, during the *Navaratri* days. The queen with Suketu reached Panchavati and worshipped the goddess Durga very devoutly. First Suketu was restored to perfect health ; then she gave birth to a son whom Angiras named Suryapratapa. This prince in due course became very powerful. He defeated his enemies and got back his kingdom and reinstated his father in it. The current belief is that every one will attain his object by the *Sarasvati puja*, as Suvedi did by the observance of this *puja*.

By the non-Brahmans, this *puja* is called the *Ayudha puja*—the worship of the implements by the artisans—or the tool-feast. Thus the Brahman worships his books and the artisan his tools.

15. The Mahasivaratri

IT is the name of a Hindu festival observed in honour of Siva, one of the gods of the Hindu Trinity. This falls generally in the month of Magha and the festival is called the *Mahasivaratri* as it is observed on the night preceding the new moon. Not only the night but the day also preceding the new moon in that month is devoted by the Smarta sect of the Hindus to Siva's worship. On this day the orthodox Hindu rises early in the morning, bathes and attends most devoutly to his prayers. He attends a temple if there is one near. Fasting, as a general rule, is observed throughout the day and the night. Sitting up in wakefulness throughout the night entirely absorbed in worshipping Siva is considered most meritorious. There are special prayers for each of the four watches (*Jamas*—three hours' duration) of the night, and the devotee who goes through these prayers on the night sacred to Siva is considered to be working his way up to oneness with Siva after his death.

The *Sivaratri* is also held sacred for the making of holy ashes by the Smartas. Holy ashes are a daily necessity to this class of Hindus, and those prepared on the day sacred to Siva are considered to be very pure. The process is extremely simple. There are certain days in the year which are held sacred for drying up cow-dung balls, from which holy ashes are made. The balls thus prepared are taken to an open yard of the house on the *Sivaratri* night and placed in the midst of a large heap of husk or chaff. The master of the house or the household priest, who had been observing a fast and repeating prayers the whole day, sets fire to this heap in the early part of the *Sivaratri* night. The heap continues in flames throughout the night and is reduced to ashes the next morning. The latter is then collected and preserved as holy ashes for use till the next *Sivaratri*.

The origin of the sacredness of the *Sivaratri* is related in the following Puranic legend:—In a forest, unknown to the public, on the Himalaya mountains there once lived a hunter with his wife and an only child in a humble cottage. He was in the habit of going out daily in the morning with his bow and arrows and returning home in the evening with some game or other which furnished the food for the whole family. As usual he went out in search of game on a certain morning. It was an unusually hot day and he wandered throughout the forest, but was not able to secure any game. The evening was fast approaching. Darkness had almost set in. Thinking it was no use lingering longer in the dense forest he turned his course towards his cottage with a melancholy countenance, for, what could his wife and child do for their supper that night? This was his sole thought. Sometimes he would stop on his way and say to himself that there was no use in going home without any flesh to cook. He saw a big tank on his way, "Ah! to be sure some animal or other must come to this tank to drink water. I shall hide myself behind some thick bush and wait for the occasion." On second thoughts, he considered it safer to climb a tree to be beyond the reach of any beast of prey. To attract beasts to the side of the tree on which he was resting he kept dropping tender leaves from the tree. He was not disappointed in his manœuvres. During the first watch of the night a doe antelope, after drinking water in the tank, approached the tree to feed at the tempting leaves without any idea of the danger that hung over-head. The hunter glad at heart hastily prepared himself to take aim at the poor beast. The antelope perceived the danger and instead of running away, most piteously addressed the hunter in human voice, "O! Hunter dear! Do not kill me now." The hunter, though startled to hear the animal speak in human voice, said, mustering up his courage: "My charming antelope! I cannot but kill you at once. My wife and child are dying at home from hunger. You must be their food to-night." "Even so, hunter, I have a dear husband and an affectionate child at home. I must take leave of them before I fall down dead by your shaft. For their sake save me for only a few hours. You are not a hard-hearted bachelor. As you feel for your wife and child, surely you must realise what my misery will be if I do not take leave of my lord and child before I lay down my life." The hunter, moved at the piteous words of the beast, thought within himself how hard-hearted he was to resolve to kill a beast so that he may feed on its carcase. But kill he must if he should eke out his livelihood in that forest. The antelope promised to return after taking leave of her husband and her child. He permitted her to do so and she promised to be back in the fourth watch of the night.

The first watch of the night was almost over. Our hero was wide awake. Having lost his first opportunity that night, he waited for another beast to approach his tree. And his heart leapt with joy at the sight of another beast approaching the tree during the second watch. He again prepared himself to aim his shaft at it. He was again astonished when he heard that antelope also begging him in human voice. Again there was a conversation, in the course of which the hunter learnt that the second antelope was the husband of the first one. It also requested the hunter to spare it till the fourth watch of the night, as it wanted to see its wife and child. The hunter gladly granted the request; for, he was sure of carrying away both these beasts at the fourth watch. He thought that beasts which argued in such an honest fashion would never prove untrue. During the third watch our hero met a third antelope, which happened to be the child of the first two antelopes. This beast also astonished the hunter by a similar request, which of course was readily granted, to be spared till the fourth watch of the night.

Thus the three watches of the night were spent by the hunter in strict wakefulness. He had not had even a wink of sleep. The tree on which he lodged for the night happened to be the *Bilva* tree (*cratæva religiosa*) the leaves of which are held to be sacred to Siva; and in dropping the leaves he was unwittingly offering worship to Siva throughout the night, for the leaves happened to fall on a ruined image of Siva which lay under the branches of that tree. To add to the hunter's fortune, the night on which all these things took place happened to be a *Sivaratri* night, though the hunter was ignorant of it. The three watches were over. The hunter was anxiously waiting for the return of the three antelopes as they promised to do. The fourth watch also was running out fast. Still the beasts never came back. The hunter had almost set himself down for a fool for having let the animals go in the first instance. The morning twilight had almost appeared. He turned his face towards the east and a most heart-rending sight met his eyes. There he saw in the dusk of the early morning the three honest animals each weeping at the fate of the other two, unmindful of its own. Even the hunter's hard heart melted away at what he saw. He turned to the other side to hide his tears; but he saw there his wife and child, who after spending the whole night in the forest in his search came running towards him in joy when they saw him. He turned again his eyes towards the east with something in his mind more noble and elevated than hitherto. He had almost resolved to excuse the beasts and give back their lives though they had not returned to him yet. But just as the lord of the day was making his appearance on the horizon, there stood before the hunter a divine *vimana* which carried away all the six—the three antelopes, the hunter, his wife and child—to the heavens—to the realm of Siva. In connection with this marvellous passing away to heaven of the beasts, the hunter and his family is held the popular belief that *Mrigasira*—the fifth lunar mansion containing three stars in Orion and figured by an antelope's head, which appear in the heavens is a symbolic representation of this Puranic story.

16. The Srijayanti or Krishnashtami

LORD KRISHNA'S birthday, *Srijayanti* or *Krishnashtami*, is the most popular festival in the whole of India. These two are the names by which this festival is called by the Vaishnavas, while among the Smartas it is known as *Gokulashtami*, and in Northern India as *Janmashtami*. By whatever name it may be known, this festive celebration of the birth of Lord Krishna is kept as a holy day by all Hindus throughout India. According to the *Puranas*, Krishna was born on the 8th lunar day (*Ashtami*) of the waning moon of the month of *Sravana* at midnight, upon the moon's entrance into *Rohini* asterism. On account of this sacred occasion a fast is held on the day preceding the date of his birth, the fast being broken as usual by a feast on the following day. The observance of the fast varies with different sects. The followers of the *Smriti*—Smartas—commence their fast with the commencement of the lunation whenever that takes place; the Vaishnavas and the Madhvas regulate their fast by the moon's passage through the asterism of *Rohini.*

Krishna is the most popular deity throughout the whole of India and is considered as the eighth *Avatar* or incarnation of Vishnu, one of the Hindu Trinity, and the following is a brief account of Krishna's history as collected from the several *Puranas.*

In days gone by there reigned in Mathura, the modern Muttra, a most wicked and unpopular king, named Kamsa, who had a cousin named Devaki married to Vasudeva, of the lunar race. On the date of the latter's marriage, Kamsa, the tyrant, drove the car in which Devaki and Vasudeva were conducted in procession. As the procession was passing along the streets an unknown voice deep as thunder came from above. "Oh you fool, Kamsa! The eighth child of the lady in the car that you are now driving will put an end to your atrocious life." As soon as Kamsa heard this ominous voice, he became greatly enraged and attempted to put Devaki to death thereby preventing the possibility of the birth of his future enemy. But

Vasudeva argued with the tyrant and pacified him by promising to deliver into his hands all the children that Devaki may bring forth. Kamsa satisfied with this assurance desisted from putting his threat into execution, and true to his promise Vasudeva handed over to Kamsa's custody the first six children that were born to Devaki. Balarama, the seventh child of Devaki, was saved by divine interference and Krishna was the eighth son. Of course Kamsa had placed strict guard throughout the palace to prevent the eighth son from being in any way saved. How then was Krishna saved? Vasudeva, as soon as the eighth child was born, took it and went out. The guards placed over the place were all charmed by *Yoganidra*—a kind of hypnotic sleep. Rain was pouring down in torrents that night, and to protect the baby from the heavy rain, Sesha, the many-headed serpent, followed Vasudeva and spread his hood over the child's head. The Jumna was flowing full and it had to be crossed. Though the river was usually deep and dangerous with whirlpools the waters at that time went down, running only knee deep. Thus by divine favour the several obstacles were overcome and the other side of the river was reached. There was a cowherd there named Nanda, whose wife Yasoda had brought to bed a female child. Vasudeva placed his son in the daughter's place, while Yasoda was also under the spell of magic sleep, and quickly returned home carrying away the female child. When Yasoda awoke she found that she had been delivered of a son and she rejoiced at it.

Yasoda's female child was now placed by Vasudeva in the bed of Devaki, no suspicions being aroused in anybody's mind. The guards who were set to watch by Kamsa were awakened by the cry of the new-born babe and starting up they sent word at once to their master. Kamsa immediately repaired to the mansion of Vasudeva and seized hold of the infant. In vain did Devaki entreat him to spare her child; but the tyrant ruthlessly dashed it against a stone, when lo! it rose into the sky and expanded into a gigantic form and laughed aloud, striking terror into the on-lookers, and addressed Kamsa in a thundering voice—"What avails it thee, Kamsa, to have thus dashed me down with the belief that thy enemy is destroyed? *He* is born that shall kill thee, the mighty one amongst the gods." Thus saying the being vanished.

Kamsa was greatly alarmed. He called a big council and ordered active search to be made for whatever young children there may be on earth and ordered that every boy in whom they observed signs of unusual vigour be put to death without any remorse. Notwithstanding all these precautions, Balarama and Krishna were growing up at the abode of Nanda, where they were roaming in the woods and joining in the sports of herdsmen's sons and daughters. When he attained to Man's estate Krishna proceeded to Gujarat, built Dvaraka and transferred to that place all the inhabitants of Muttra, after killing Kamsa in a combat.

Krishnashtami is the festival which is celebrated in honour of the birthday of Krishna. At about midnight, on the *Ashtami* night (September 8th), a clay image of Krishna in the form of a baby is made in every Hindu house and worshipped. Several dishes of sweets are offered to the god, to be consumed afterwards by the inmates of the house. Apart from its importance from a religious point of view the feast is very popular with Hindu children on account of the sweets that are distributed to them on the occasion. A superstitious belief is current amongst the Hindus that as Krishna, who was born in the asterism of *Rohini*, was the cause of the death of his maternal uncle Kamsa, the birth of a male child in that asterism forbodes evil to the maternal uncle of that child; and there were instances in old days in which such children were put to death. But this superstitious belief is fast dying out.

17. The Varalakshmi Worship

LAKSHMI, the bride of Vishnu, is represented as the goddess of Prosperity and abundance as also of Love and Beauty, in the Hindu Mythology: the designation of *vara* indicates the power, generally credited to her, of granting boons to her devotees. A day is specially set apart for her special worship. The evening is both a religious and festive occasion to the Hindu ladies and children, and soon after sunset the Varalakshmi is worshipped in every Hindu household on a large scale with flowers, food, puddings and sweets of several kinds. A figure of the Goddess of Prosperity is painted on a brass or copper vessel and placed in the hall or court of the house under a small leafy canopy erected for the occasion. The Brahman priest is invited to repeat the form of the worship and the oldest married lady of the house who has observed a fast during the whole day performs the *puja* of Varalakshmi, soon after sunset, with sincere devotion. The priest receives his fees and then the eager children partake of the puddings and sweetmeats first offered to the goddess during the course of the worship. The several *Puranas* speak highly of the powers of Lakshmi, who is represented as the essence of wealth and prosperity and the mother of the universe, eternal and imperishable. As Vishnu is supposed to be all-pervading, so also is Lakshmi considered to be omnipresent. Vishnu is understanding, Lakshmi is intellect; Vishnu is desire, and Lakshmi is wish. He is meaning; she is speech. She is the moon, the unfading light, the moving principle of the whole world. She is represented to have sprung from the waves of the milk ocean, when it was churned by the demons and the gods seated on a full-blown lotus and holding a water-lily (*nilotpala*) in her hand and radiant with beauty. As soon as she was observed to rise up, heavenly musicians sang sweet songs and celestial nymphs danced. The holy Ganges and other sacred river goddesses attended for her ablutions. The elephants of the skies, taking up their pure waters in gold vases, poured them over her—the queen of the world.

The ocean of milk presented her with a wreath of never-fading flowers and the artist of the gods decorated her with heavenly jewels and gems. The picture of Lakshmi is generally drawn thus in this night's worship—with the goddess seated on a full-blown lotus, elephants on both sides pouring water over her from gold vases lifted up in their trunks, &c. After Lakshmi was thus bathed, attired and adorned, she cast herself on the breast of Hari—Vishnu—and became his bride ever since that time. Rudra, the chief of the gods, extolled her powers as soon as she sprang out of the ocean and called her the mother of all beings, the superhuman power incarnate, and the purifier of the universe. Lakshmi to a Hindu is the presiding deity of Prosperity, and her worship is deemed to bring good fortune in every household.

The following account of Lakshmi is from the *Ramayana* translated by R. T. H. Griffiths :—

> " When many a year had fled
> Up floated, on her lotus bed,
> A maiden fair, and tender-eyed,
> In the young flush of beauty's pride.
> She shone with pearl and golden sheen,
> And seals of glory stamped her queen.

On each round arm glowed many a gem,
On her smooth brows a diadem.
Rolling in waves beneath her crown,
The glory of her hair rolled down.
Pearls on her neck of price untold,
The lady shone like burnished gold.
Queen of the gods, she leapt to land,
A lotus in her perfect hand,
And fondly, of the lotus sprung,
To lotus-bearing Vishnu clung.
Her, gods above and men below
As Beauty's Queen and Fortune know."

18. The Vinayaka Chaturthi

VINAYAKA CHATURTHI day is set apart for the sole worship of Ganesa, the common deity of all Hindus. As he is supposed to be very fond of rice puddings, these dishes are cooked on a very large scale in every Hindu house and offered to the god, to be consumed, by the members of the family, after the worship is over. A fresh image of Ganesa in clay is made and worshipped on this day. One hundred and eight different names of this god are repeated after the preliminary ceremonies and 108 different flowers are thrown in worship over him. The origin of this worship is prehistoric. Yudhisthira, the hero of the *Mahabharata*, Damayanti, the queen of the Nishada King Nala, Indra, the Lord of the Heavens and even Krishna, the expounder of the *Bhagavatgita* are said to have devoutly worshipped Ganesa and to have obtained their desired ends. Vinayaka or Ganesa is the eldest son of Siva and Parvati, or of Parvati only, according to the following legend, as he sprang from the scarf of her body. Siva had gone from home and Parvati was left alone on the Kailasa; she wished to have a bath and not liking the idea of any person entering the house then, she rubbed her body with her hands and from the dirt that rolled off produced a figure to which she gave life and named Ganesa. She then asked Ganesa to sit at the door and allow no one, whoever he might be, to come in till she had finished her bath. Ganesa sat at his duty and while Parvati was bathing inside, Siva returned home. He wanted to enter his house, but Ganesa would not allow him. After trying in vain to persuade him with gentle words, the great god used threats which, however, had no effect. He was at last compelled to cut off Ganesa's head and force his way in. When the goddess who was within perceived her lord entering and when she came to know that Ganesa had been murdered, she would not speak to Siva until her attendant was restored to life. In order to do this, Siva gave orders to his army of the Bhutaganas to find the first living creature that slept with its head turned towards the north, to cut off its head and to fit it into Ganesa's body. The Bhutas searched and searched for a very long time and at last found an elephant asleep with its head to the north and cutting off its head they brought it and fixed it to Ganesa's body, and lo! he rose up a man in body and elephant in face. This story also accounts for the belief of the Hindus to avoid the northern aspect in sleep.

Vinayaka is the eldest son of Siva and Parvati and one of the most popular of the deities of India. He is the male Minerva and the Janus of public ways. His shrine is in every Hindu village. He is worshipped in every Hindu house. Every school boy commences his lessons after giving his usual prayers to Vinayaka. Every merchant commences his operations after first propitiating this deity. In marriages and in every kind of religious ceremony, Vinayaka is the first god whose help is invoked. Almost all the standard works in Sanskrit and the Vernacular languages begin with an invocation of the help of Ganesa. Vinayaka's figure is represented as elephant in face and man in body. The elephant's head is regarded as the emblem of sagacity. In his image he is always seated at his ease, with his legs folded under him on a lotus throne. He has four arms and they hold an elephant's trunk, a noose, a mace, and a *modaka* (rice pudding). He wears a crown. His ears are adorned with jewels and his forehead wears the *vibhuti*—the sacred ashes. He wears a garland of pearls and precious stones round his neck. He is worshipped under the different names of Vinayaka, Ganesa, Ganapati, Pillaiyar, etc. As this most popular deity is worshipped in almost every village, there is a belief among certain people that he is the god of the Sudras and lower orders, who are generally uneducated. As an authority for this belief, the following couplet is sometimes quoted :—

Vipranam daivatam Sambhuh
Kshatriyanam tu Madhavah
Vaisyanam tu bhaved Brahma
Sudranam Gananayakah ||

The above verse means that Siva is the god of the Brahmans, Vishnu of the Kshatriyas, Brahma of the Vaisyas, and Ganesa of the Sudras. This is a most fanciful verse, which is not at all corroborated by any other authority. If any regard is to be paid to this couplet, then no Brahman can worship Vishnu and no Vaisya can worship Siva, facts which are absurd on their very face, as tested by both the ancient and modern ways of Hindu faith.

Ganesa worship is a prehistoric one and it goes without saying that the couplet sometimes quoted as an authority that Ganesa is the god of the Sudras is most unfounded. On the other hand, he is worshipped by the highest class of Brahmans. There are also special sects who are called Ganapatiyas, whose sole devotion is to this deity. Vinayaka is the deity that rules over good and bad alike—controlling the evil in every case and preventing hindrances and difficulties. As such, he is the embodiment of success and of all those qualities in short which overcome hindrances in every undertaking and of their usual accompaniments—good living, plenty, prosperity, and peace. This is the one great and real reason for the popularity of the worship of this deity.

There is always a small shrine of Vignesvara, attached to all Siva temples. In the Vishnu temples too he is worshipped as *Tumbikkai-*

alvar—the sage of the elephant's trunk—and as *Vishvaksena.* Sometimes he has his own temples too. As he is the favourite son of Siva, he receives honours equal to Siva. His image is with sincere devotion adored by men and women alike. He is supposed to represent the several personifications of sagacity, shrewdness, patience, and learning. As a test of his wisdom, it is related that when he was a child and playing in company with his brother Subrahmanya, Siva promised to present a mango-fruit to him who made a circuit round the world and returned first. Subrahmanya summoned his peacock, mounted it and was ready for the journey. But Ganesa calmly went round Siva, his father, and demanded the fruit. "But you never went round the world," said Siva. "What is the world, but your own holy self? I went round you. *Ergo*, I went round the world," was Ganesa's wise reply. Siva was of course convinced, praised Ganesa for his shrewdness, and gave him the promised fruit, which however, he shared with Subrahmanya. The peculiarity of this deity is that his worship is combined as it were with that of every other god. All sects unite in claiming him as their own. It is for this reason that his shrines are found generally associated with those of other deities—Siva and Vishnu. The largest temple built solely in honour of Ganesa in India is the Uchchippillaiyar temple on the top of the famous and beautiful rock at Trichinopoly.

Though this god is invoked on several occasions during the year, there is a special day in every year which is set apart particularly for his worship, and this day is called the *Vinayaka Chaturthi* day, which falls on the fourth lunar day of the bright half of the month of Simha. The Tamils term this day *Pillaiyar Chavutti* day.

Of all the figures in the Hindu Mythology, that of Ganesa or Pillaiyar must be most familiar to every European. In the bathing ghat of every river and underneath the pipal tree will be seen a figure in a sitting posture, short and stout, with a protuberant stomach and four hands, riding a mouse and with the body of a man and the head of an elephant. This is the image Ganesa or Pillaiyar, and there is not a single village in the whole of India which does not possess at least half a dozen of these familiar images. The elephant head has only one tusk in full and the other appears cut off in the middle, which is supposed to have resulted in a scuffle between Ganesa and Parasurama. The "belly-god" is on this account called *Ekadanta*, or the single-tusked. Ganesa is said to have written the *Mahabharata* at the dictation of Vyasa—for it is said that the latter was so quick in repeating the epic that no mortal could have managed to follow him.

19. The Hindu New Year's Day

EVERY nation in the world has its New Year's Day. A year is the time of the apparent revolution of the sun through the ecliptic ; and a sidereal year is the time in which the sun departing from any fixed star returns to the same. The Hindu's astronomical year is sidereal. He calls it *Samvatsaradi*, the first day of the year or the *Vishu-chaitravishu*, the equinoctical point of Aries, into which the sun enters at the vernal equinox. This event generally falls on the 12th April and is considered by the Hindu a *punaykala*—a holy occasion. So on the New Year's Day the Manes and Gods are propitiated by offerings of *tarpana*—oblations of water—and other allied ceremonies. In other respects, the New Year's Day is a day of feasting.

Though thus the astronomical Hindu year falls on the 12th April, the New Year's Day is observed on different days by different sects of the Hindus, according as they happen to follow the lunar, the luni-solar or the solar calendar. The Tamils follow the solar, and their year is thus the sidereal year. The Telugus and the Canarese follow the *Chandra-mana* reckoning, and their year is the luni-solar, which begins earlier than the 12th April. The Malayalis follow the Tamils, though their *Kollamandu*—which is more an agricultural year—begins about the middle of September, when the sun enters the autumnal equinox.

On the New Year Day the elderly people—males and females—take a sacred bath in the holy rivers or the sea, whichever happens to be nearest. The males propitiate the Manes and the deities; children appear in their holiday dress and jewels. The nearest temple is attended and the god in it is worshipped. In some families children and other members receive new cloths. A sumptuous meal is cooked in every house and poor relations are always cordially invited to the feast. At evening time the *Panchanga* or the Calendar of the New Year is read out and expounded by a holy Brahman. Several people assemble to listen to this exposition. At the end of this ceremony, *attar*, *pan supari*, and dessert are distributed. Sometimes a short entertainment of music is also added to this ceremony. The whole day is spent more or less in mirth and festivity and a light supper closes the day's proceedings.

In Malabar, the New Year's Day festivities are observed on a very grand scale. On New Year's eve all the gold coins available in the house, all gold jewels, all kinds of auspicious fruits and flowers and everything considered to be good to look at are placed in the room set apart for the worship of the family god. The Karnavan who is the head of the family first opens this room between 4 and 5 on New Year's morn and worships with a lighted lamp in his hand all these articles. Then every member of the house one after the other goes to the front of the room with his or her eyes shut and opens them when arrived at the proper spot to take a sight of the auspicious articles collected. The Karnavan—head of the family—presents each with something or other,—coins, jewels, flowers, fruits, etc. This is the chief difference between the Malayalis and other Hindus as regards the observance of the New Year's festivities. And every Hindu takes care to see an auspicious sight on the New Year's morn whether he is a Malayali or other Hindu.

20. The Onam Feast in Malabar

THE *Onam* is the oldest of the national feasts of Malabar. This feast commences nine days previous to *Onam* day from the *Hasta* asterism and lasts three days after it. The commencement of the festivities is announced by the youngsters twanging a bow-string which is called *Villukkottal.* This *Villukkottal* is very harsh but is carried on throughout the continuance of the feast for ten days. It corresponds to the sounding of harsh drums by the low-caste people of the Madras Coast during the *Sankramana* festivities—the entrance of the sun into the sign Capricorn. The *Onam* is celebrated to commemorate the reign of Mahabali, the mythological king who is said to have ruled over Malabar. He is reported to have been humbled by Vishnu in Tirukkakarai, a sacred town in Travancore, where Vishnu appeared as a fair young boy weeping. The Hindu legends put this appearance down as the *Vamanavatara* or the dwarf incarnation of Vishnu; but the homely Malayali prefers to describe him as a fair boy. Mahabali asked the boy what he wanted and gave him fruits and sweetmeats, but the cunning young rogue would accept nothing. "What do you want, then?" asked the king who used to give all those who came to him whatever they asked for. The boy said that he required only three feet of ground and this was readily granted by the unsuspecting king. Suddenly the boy assumed a huge shape (generally called *Visvarupa* or world-pervading shape) and with one foot covered all Mahabali's dominions. The second foot took in all the sky covering the king's dominions, but where was the third foot of ground? The king was amazed and thought that Vishnu himself was before him. "Where am I to measure the third foot?" cried the deity. "On my head, my lord!" was the calm reply of the monarch. And so it came to pass, and Mahabali was humbled to dust. This event took place on the *Onam* day, in the asterism of *Tiru-Ona* (whence the name *Oṇa*, devoid of, *Tiru* which means holy) in the month of *Simha* answering to the latter half of August and the former half of September.

But a question may arise here as to why this day which is a sorrowful day on which a good sovereign died should be observed with festivities. It is stated that Mahabali requested Vishnu that the day of his departure to the other world should be observed with festivities and the boon, it is said, was granted by the deity. There is also another belief. On the *Onam* day, king Mahabali is supposed to again pay a visit to his country, his object being to see whether his subjects still enjoy the same amount of happiness and prosperity, as they did under him. So, to give a right impression to their whilom sovereign, the Malayalis keep up the festivities on this day, for, if they should mourn, Mahabali would return to his abode in the other world with a grieved heart and a vexed mind.

At the approach of *Onam*, the houses in Malabar are decorated with flowers and festoons. A clay image of Vishnu is made in every home and worshipped during these ten days. The god is inaugurated with a special feast called *Puadai* feast in which rice and *nendra* plantain are cooked and offered to the god. The duty of bringing flowers and boughs to decorate the houses is left to the younger boys. Each youngster takes a small basket and proceeds to the gardens and fields with his companions merrily singing a shrill hymn called the *Onam* hymn. The following is the translation of one of the verses :—" Oh ! the moon-disc-decorated (Siva) protect me. Oh ! the husband of Parvati (Siva) protect me. Oh! the moon-faced deity protect me. Oh! the god worshipped by Indra and other gods protect me." It does not matter if Siva is extolled while flowers are being gathered for the worship of Vishnu, the rule among the youngsters being that some deity or other must be praised. The image is called Mahadeva. The women and girls at home amuse themselves with a dance in a circle called the *Tappattikkali;* all stand up and circle round and round clapping their hands and singing sweet songs in praise of Vishnu or some other deity. One of the elders of the party starts the song and leads the dancers, and the others accompany her by repeating what she says and following her movements. These amusements continue until the *Onam* when presents of new cloths are made. All the male and female members of every family, including the children, receive their new cloths from the Karnavan, or family head. The women also receive any other new cloths meant for some future occasion, as *Onam* day is considered an auspicious one for receiving such presents. Early in the morning the labourers and cultivators visit their masters with a number of *nendram kay*, a species of plantain peculiar to Malabar, and receive in return a new cloth, oil, rice, ghi, etc., as becoming their position. There is nothing unusual in the food partaken during the *Onam* festivities except that the *nendram* fruit must form one of the dishes. The house of every Nambudri Brahman is thrown open to as many Brahmans as may care to visit it. The Pandi Brahmans, or the Brahman cloth merchants from Tinnevelly who visit Malabar with the *mundu* cloth specially made for the feast in Ambasamudram and Viravanallur in the Tinnevelly District, are well fed and their cloths are largely in demand. On *Onam* day a special dish of *nendram* is partaken by every Malayali—this is called *pulukkiya pala norukka.*

After the presents have been distributed, the worship of Vishnu succeeds and the feast over, the Malayali men assemble to witness a grand sham fight (*Padakkali* or *Kayyankali*). Each of the opposing sides must be under the patronage of some influential Malayalis who, a month or two before the *Onam* feast agree to conclude it in this, the usual way. This entertainment is a very costly one. The men engaged to fight are generally well-known wrestlers and acrobats; they live at the expense of the person who engages them, and are specially trained in order to display their full skill on the *Onam* day. All the people assemble to witness the sports—men, boys and little girls, the women stopping at home to dance and sing the *Tappattikali*. The men divide themselves into two parties, or *cheries*, and sit on the ground in rows, 15 to 20 yards being left between them and here it is that the combatants display their skill. Two men are chosen as umpires on each side. The game commences at 1 o'clock every day and continues until 6 P.M. on *Onam* day and the two succeeding days, and at 6 P.M. on the 10th day of the feast—*i.e.*, the third day from *Onam* proper which is also the third day after the commencement of the sports—the decision of the umpires is declared. A commencement is made by one party sending out ten boys to challenge ten boys from the other side. These display their strength and agility of limb by acrobatic feats, and then challenge the boys from the other party. The latter accepts the challenge by sending out ten boys to meet them. Both the sides return to their respective seats. The umpires then call out by name one boy from one party and ask him whether he would fight so and so, on the other side. Sometimes the boy accepts, sometimes he sneeringly says that it would be a disgrace on his part to be matched against such a poor and weak opponent. The doubts are decided by the umpires and the fight takes place. Certain conditions are agreed upon and woe betide him who disregards them. The conditions are whether the blows to be struck shall be all on the back (*odaram*), on the sides (*kadakam*), on the back of the neck (*pedani*), on the cheek (*chekadatta*), etc. The youngsters then set to, two at a time, and an account is carefully kept by the umpires of successes and defeats. Then in gradation of age, dexterity and skill, others, still two and two at a time, one from each party, appear and fight. This goes on for three days. On the last day the decision of the umpires is given. Every one, specially engaged for the entertainment, is rewarded on the night of the third day, in accordance with his powers and prowess. This closes the *padakkali* which takes place before a Rajah or local chieftain, now a rich *tarawad*, who witnesses the whole scene and distributes the prizes. It is considered a high honour to win a prize in the *padakkali*. Generally no harm is done in the sham fight, but sometimes, under excitement, and when the parties attacking each other are professional wrestlers or bear a grudge towards one another accidents do occur. This whole sham fight is called *onitalla*. But these are rare and never come into Court, for king Mahabali cannot thus be insulted. On the evening of the last day the clay image of Vishnu is placed on an ornamental plank made of jack-wood and with much tamasha, in which the young and the old freely join, is taken to a river, tank or some unfrequented place, and thrown away. From time immemorial the *Onam* seems to have been celebrated in the same festive way in Malabar.

Several treaties, engagements and papers of importance edited by Mr. Logan, late of the Madras Civil Service—the greatest authority in Malabar matters—contain allusions to this *Onam*, so remote as in A.D. 1784.

APPENDIX A.

The Kaliyuga

[We are enabled to place before our readers to-day* an admirable article on the Kaliyuga from the pen of a learned Hindu gentleman. The word "Kaliyuga" is constantly cropping up in native writings and speeches, and is likely to do so still more in the future, but a perusal of this article will explain the belief, for a superstition it cannot fairly be called, based as it is on writings held sacred by the people. That extraordinary divine, Dr. Cumming, used to startle periodically worthy British matrons and susceptible young men and maidens by proving to his and their complete satisfaction that the end of the world was near at hand. His prophecies were the result of abstruse mathematical calculations based on his interpretation of certain scriptural texts; but, so far as we are aware, he never brought forward such strong evidence as is furnished in the Puranic writings which fixes the exact hour of the dawn of the Last Day at 2 A.M. on the 25th November, 1899. The point, however, on which particular stress is to be laid is the difficulty that must naturally exist in dealing with people who

---

* The *Madras Mail*, 19th November, 1896.

honestly believe in this Kaliyuga story during such a crisis as the present. Even the most sceptical will read with some surprise of the evils accompanying the close of this age, as described in the *Vishnu Purana*. They tally so closely with recent changes in the social order of Hindu life.—EDITOR, *The Madras Mail.*]

A *Yuga* in Sanskrit (in Heb. *Olim*, in Gr. *Aion*, and in Lat. *Ævum*) means an age of the world. Four *Yugas* are recognised by the Hindu mythology, the *Krita*, the *Treta*, the *Dvapara* and the *Kali*. All these four *Yugas* joined together constitute a great age, or an aggregate of four ages (*Mahayuga*). A thousand such aggregates are a day of Brahma. Let us give the number of years allotted to each *Yuga* in the years of the gods and in the years of men. The first rule is that a year of men is equal to a day of the gods. The following table gives the years of the four *Yugas* according to both these calculations:—

Yugas.		Divine years.	Years of Mortals.
Krita	...	4,800	4,800×360=1,728,000
Treta	...	3,600	3,600×360=1,296,000
Dvapara	...	2,400	2,400×360= 864,000
Kali	...	1,200	1,200×360= 432,000
			Total (a Mahayuga) 4,320,000

So the notion of these four ages may be best remembered by a deteriorating series expressed by a descending arithmetical progression as 4, 3, 2, 1, by the conversion of units into thousands and by the legend that these are divine years each composed of 360 years of men. A period of 4,320,000 years constitutes a great age, or a *Mahayuga*, and this number multiplied by 1,000 *i.e.*, 4,320,000,000 years becomes a day of Brahma:—

Daivikanam Yuganam tu sahasram parisamkhyaya | *Brahmam-ekamaharjneyam tavati ratrir-eva cha.* At the end of this day a dissolution of the universe will occur, when all the three worlds, earth and the regions of space will all be consumed by fire. The three worlds then become but one mighty ocean. Brahma will sleep for a night, of equal duration with his day, on this ocean and at its close will create the world anew. A year of Brahma is composed of 360 such days and nights and a hundred such years constitute his whole life, which is called a *Kalpa. Brahmanaschayusha Kalpa kalpavidbhih nirupitah.* Such, in brief, is the belief of the Hindus regarding the ages and the duration of the world and full details of this belief will be found in Books I, IV, V and VI of the *Vishnu Purana*.

What is the object of Brahma in thus destroying the whole universe and recreating it? The Hindu philosophy most beautifully explains it:—

> 'Sarva-bhutani Kaunteya
> Prakritam yanti mamikam |
> Kalpa-kshaye punas-tani
> Kalpadau visrijamy-aham ||

"I absorb the whole universe in myself at the end of the *Kalpa* and at its commencement I create it again," says Brahma. Volumes are written in the several *Puranas* about the merits and demerits of each *Yuga*, or age. The brief way to remember the whole subject would be to imagine Virtue to have four legs. In the *Krita*, or the first *Yuga*, Virtue walks on all her four legs. In the *Treta*, or the second *Yuga*, she walks only on three of her legs; in the *Dvapara* on two, and in the last age, the *Kaliyuga*, on only one leg. After this brief remark about the Hindu notions of the age of the universe, its destruction and recreation, let us confine ourselves on the present occasion to the full description of the *Kaliyuga*, the fourth Hindu age which is current now, and in which Virtue is said to walk only on one of her four legs. The *Kaliyuga* era commenced in 3102 B. C. and we are now in the year 4998 of the *Kaliyuga ; i.e.*, 4,997 years of the *Kaliyuga* have already passed away and the year current 4998 commenced on the 12th April, 1896. The year 5000 of the *Kaliyuga* will commence on the 12th April 1899, A.D. and end on the 11th April 1900. The belief of the orthodox Hindus from the Himalayas to Cape Comorin that this, their fourth, era is one of vice, wickedness and misery is universal, and is recorded in almost each and every one of their *Puranas.* It is also strongly believed that the year 5000 of the *Kaliyuga* will be a year of doom and ruin. Let us dwell at length on both these beliefs.

In Book IV of the *Vishnu Purana* it is stated that Kali feared to set his feet on this world as long as it was purified by the touch of the sacred feet of Krishna.

> Yâvat sapâda padmâbhyâm
> Sprisan-âste Ramâpatih |
> Tâvat Kalir vai prithivîm
> Parâkrântum na ch-âsakat ||

The usual notion of the Hindus is that the age of Kali set in from the death of Krishna; but it is also a common supposition that it commenced a little later, with the reign of Parikshit. It is said in Book II. of the *Bhagavata* that after Krishna died or ascended to his abode in Heaven, the Pandavas also followed him after installing their grandson and heir, Parikshit, as the Emperor of the *Bharata*. The new monarch, according to the usual custom, set out on a tour round his empire to establish order, to make friends with friendly kings and to subdue vassals. He finished his tour and was returning to his capital, when, on his way back and near the river Sarasvati he noticed that a cow and an ox were being tortured to death by a person who appeared to be a Sudra, and who had put on royal robes. The cruel Sudra had cut off three of the four legs of the ox and was proceeding to cut off the fourth leg also. The cow appeared to be only a bag of bones; she was so lean and dried up by starvation. Even a heart of adamant would have melted away at the sight. But the Sudra went on kicking and lashing her incessantly. Parikshit was horrified at what he saw and in great wrath addressed the person as follows:—"Who are you, vile wretch, that have put on royal garments? Are you not ashamed of your conduct towards these poor creatures, one of which you have already deprived of its three legs and the other you have starved to death? I must put you at once to death." The Emperor then asked the ox and the cow to relate their history. After some reluctance the ox said that he was Justice (or Virtue, *Dharma*) who walked on his four legs of (1) contemplation upon God, (2) purity of life, (3) mercy towards living beings, and (4) truth in the *Krita yuga* or first Hindu age; that he had lost his three legs at the rate of one at the end of every *Yuga* and that he had his only leg, truth, left remaining at the commencement of the Kali era and that lord of the *Kaliyuga* was already aiming at his fourth leg. The Emperor learnt the cow to be the goddess Earth who was reduced to that condition by the departure of Krishna from this world of men. Parikshit was horrified at what he saw and heard, and aimed his death-dealing sword at the Sudra, when, wonder of wonders! he threw away his royal garments, assumed his true form and falling down before the Emperor, begged for his life. This Sudra was Kali himself. Parikshit was a true hero and a genuine sprout of the Pandava family. His motto was, never kill a fallen enemy. So he spared Kali's life on condition that he left his dominions at once. But Kali begged for some place to live in. He was asked by the Emperor to find his abode in gambling houses, in taverns, in women of unchaste lives, in slaughtering places and in gold. And Kali agreed to do so. So, as long as Parikshit reigned over the Bharata (India) Kali confined himself only to these five places; but after the reign of that just Emperor, Kali made his way to other places like wild fire and established his power throughout the length and breadth of the whole world. This, in short, is the legend of the setting in of the *Kaliyuga*.

In India when a young boy or girl happens to break, in eating or dress, the orthodox rules of caste, his or her parents will say: "O! It is all the result of the *Kaliyuga*." If a Hindu becomes a convert to any other religion, or if any atrocious act is committed the Hindu will observe: "O! It is the ripening of Kali." Every deviation from the established custom, every vice, every crime, in fact everything wicked, is set down by the ordinary Hindu to the ascending power of the Lord of the Kali age. These notions entertained by the people must not be entirely set down to be wholly superstitious. In every one of the Hindu *Puranas* the *Kaliyuga* (or the dark age) is described as the worst period of everything wrong, unhappy or miserable. The *Vishnu Purana*, *Bhagavata*, *Devibhagavata*, and a number of religious works give a glowing description of the numerous miseries reserved for mankind in the *Kaliyuga*, and the ordinary Hindu bred up from his infancy in the *Puranic* lore has accepted these beliefs as part and parcel of his existence, and anything going wrong in his own household or round about him is set down to the influence of the Kali age. Parasara describes the evils of *Kaliyuga* in detail in the *Vishnu Purana*. We will give some of the most prominent ones here:—The strict rules of caste, order and observances will never exist. The rights enjoined by the four *Vedas* will perish. The rules of conduct between the husband and wife between the preceptor and his disciple will be disregarded. Marriage rules will be set at naught. Every book will be a sacred book. All gods will be gods. People will turn proud at small possessions. Wives will desert their husbands when the latter become poor and take up to persons who are rich. A person possessing money will be the lord of everything, irrespective of his birth or position in life. All money will be spent on mere show. The world will become avaricious. Men will desire to acquire wealth by dishonest means. Cows will be fed only as long as they supply milk. The people will ever remain in fear of famine and scarcity. They will ever be watching the sky for a drop of rain. Severe famines will rage and people will be driven to the necessity of living upon leaves of trees. There will never be abundance or pleasure in the Kali age. Kings, instead of protecting their subjects, will plunder them under the pretence of levying taxes. Men of all degrees will believe themselves to be equal to the Brahmans. Everyone who happens to have cars, elephants or steeds will fancy himself to be a Rajah. There will be no warriors or Princes who could be called by such names on account of their birth. People will desert their houses. Children will die in great numbers. Women will bear children at the age of 5, 6 or 7 and men beget them when they are 8, 9 or 10. Grey hair will appear when a person is only 12 years of age and the duration of life for men will only be 20 years. The *Vedas*, the gods, the Brahmans, the sacred waters, will all be disregarded. The parents-in-law will be respected in the place of parents and brothers-in-law (brothers of wives) will be one's bosom friends. Sins will be committed daily and everything which brings down misery on human beings will be found to be prevailing to the greatest extent in the Kali age.

This is but a part of the description given in one of the greatest of the Hindu *Puranas* on the evils of the Kali age. The railway carriage where a Brahman and a non-Brahman sit side by side in the same compartment and the schools where English is taught in the same way to a Brahman as to a non-Brahman, instead of exciting the admiration of the orthodox Hindu for the benefits they have conferred upon the public, are looked upon as the platforms where Kali plays most for levelling caste distinctions. Female education, though authorities exist in the *Puranas* themselves for such a course, is viewed as another turn which Kali has taken to corrupt womankind. The several Government and Municipal taxes are considered to be the miseries of the mighty reign of Kali without the least consideration that the subject is bound to pay to the State for his own protection. The Hindu mind is ever ingenious in looking upon everything from a Kali point of view. But we must, at the same time, mention here that it is only the Hindu who lives in remote villages and who has not had the advantage of a free education who thinks thus. Every educated Hindu, of course, takes the right view of the case. Thus ends our description of the *Kaliyuga* in general and of the evils thereof as found in the *Puranas* and as prevailing among the people.

In addition to this belief there is yet another, and a strong one, that the year 5000 of the *Kaliyuga* (April 1899—April 1900) will be a year of doom and ruin. The famine that is threatening now a great portion of India, the grain riots everywhere, the failure of monsoons, the bubonic plague in Bombay, the several fires and floods in almost all the great rivers (*Mahanadis*) this year, such as the Krishna.

Godavari, Kaveri, Narmada and Tapti, which have caused immense loss of lives and property, are believed by the uneducated classes to be ushering us into a period of general cataclysms which is expected to take place in the last days of 1899 A. D. We will examine now the sources of the belief. Although all the *Puranas* are unanimous in describing the miseries of the Kali age there is fortunately only one *Purana* which speaks of the ruin of the world in the year 5000 of the Kali age. But this one *Purana* is the greatest authority to the whole of India. Its name is the *Devibhagavata* and it is regarded as a most sacred book. In the 6th chapter of Book IX it is related that the three goddesses Sarasvati, Ganga, and Lakshmi had a quarrel among themselves in heaven and each cursed the other. By the power of the curses they were converted into the rivers of Sarasvati, Ganga (Ganges) and Padmavati in this world and are expiating their sins here. Lakshmi in addition to her form as the river Padmavati has assumed also the shape of the shrub *Tulasi (Oscymum sanctum)*. In the 8th chapter it is stated that these goddesses will abandon this world in the year 5000 of the *Kaliyuga* and with the disappearance of these noble rivers everything will disappear from the world with the exception of two places —Benares and Brindavan (Muttra). The original in Sanskrit stands thus :—

> Kalau pancha-sahasram cha
> Varsham sthitva cha Bharate |
> Jagmus-tas-cha sarit rupam
> Vihaya Sri-Hareh padam || (1)
> Yani sarvani tirthani
> Kasi Brindavanam vina |
> Yasyanti sarvam tabhih cha.
> Vaikuntham ajnaya Hareh || (2)

(1) They—the goddesses Sarasvati, Ganga and Lakshmi, after having stayed in this world for 5,000 years of the *Kaliyuga* in the shape of rivers, gave up their transformed shapes and went to the abode of Vishnu (heaven).

(2) All other holy things, too, with the exception of Kasi (Benares) and Brindavan (Muttra) accompanied them to the abode of Hari by the order of Hari.

The statement contained in the above two verses is believed to be the highest authority for the impending doom in the year named. Except Benares and Brindavan, everything holy will disappear from the world. The year

5000 of the *Kaliyuga* occurs in two other places also in the *Devibhagavata*, once in the middle of Chapter 7 of Book IX when Narayana pronounces the liberation of the curse to the goddesses :—

> Kalau pancha sahasre cha
> Gate varshe cha mokshanam |

'When 5,000 years of the Kali age have expired you will be liberated from the curse.' Again in Chapter 13 (1st verse) where Narada asks Narayana to relate to him what happened to the goddesses after the year 5000, he says :—

> Kalau pancha-Sahasrabde
> Samatite Suresvara |
> Kva gata sa Mahabhaga
> Tanme vyakhyatum arhasi ||

Thus from a minute examination of the *Devibhagavata*, the year 5000 is alluded to in only three places in Chapter 8, 9 and 13 of the ninth book of that work. And it is only in Chapter 8 that the disappearance of everything from the world in the year 5000 *Kaliyuga* is alluded to. And the Hindu belief in the *Puranas* is that everything happens as predicted therein and even so the doom and ruin of the year 5000 will come to pass as foretold by the *Devibhagavata*,

In addition to the Puranic belief there are a few verses current among the astrologers of India which imply that the Hindu religion will perish in the year 5000 of the Kali age. They are as follows:—

Kalau pancha-sahasrante
Vishnuh tyakshyati medinim | (1)
Yada Vishnur-divam gachchhet
Tada Veda-viparyasah || (2)
Yada Veda-viparyasah
Tada jyotir-divam vrajet | (3)
Tasmat-tu pancha-sahasram
Phala-sastram Kalau yuge || (4)

They mean (1) Vishnu abandons this world at the close of the year 5000 of the *Kaliyuga*. (2) When Vishnu goes away, the *Vedas* will be turned upside down. (3) When the *Vedas* have suffered thus, the splendour of the planets will vanish. (4) So, the truths of astrology will be current in this world only up to the year 5000 of the *Kaliyuga*. These verses, which allude to the ruin of India three years hence, are said to have been uttered by Krishnamisra, a poet who flourished in the Court of Vikramaditya at Ujjain in the 11th Century A.D. These are the only sources for the strong Hindu belief that the year 5000 will bring general ruin to the whole world. Some are charitable in stating that if the whole world is not ruined, there will be wonderful changes and utter misery and famine at least in that year. At what time of the year 5000 will this ruin overcome India will be the next question.

In the Hindu calendar every month has a Zodiac called *Rasi* with the position of the planets for the month indicated in it by astronomical calculations. Generally not more than a single planet will be found in each of the 12 houses, or mansions, of the Zodiac. Rarely two or three or even four will be found once in several years in one and the same mansion. But if more than four of the planets are found combined in the same house a great calamity is foreseen. The following verses of the *Jyotisha Sastra* may be read with interest:—

> Pancha griha hanti samasta desan
> Shashta griha hanti samasta bhupan |
> Sapta griha hanti samasta lokan
> Nirmartyam ashta griha samyutena ||

They mean that the combination of five planets in one of the mansions of the Zodiac in any month will lead to the destruction of all countries; the combination of six planets, to the destruction of all Kings; that of seven, to the destruction of all worlds, and if eight planets combine the universe will be rendered destitute of men. Bhishma the just and the greatest warrior of the world fell in the wars of the *Mahabharata* in the month of *Magrasira* (December) on the new moon day—*Amavasa*—when seven planets combined in a single mansion of the Zodiac of that month. But for that combination such a mighty warrior would never have fallen. This is the belief of the Hindus. The year 1896 A.D., is, as we have stated already, 4998 of the *Kaliyuga* corresponding to the year *Durmukhi* of the *Brihaspati* cycle of 60 years. Five thousand *Kaliyuga* will be 1899 A.D. and the year *Vikari* of the *Brihaspati* cycle. According to the astronomical calculations of the Hindus, eight planets meet in the mansion of Scorpio (*Vrichchhika*) of the Zodiac of the month of *Krittika*, corresponding to the last week of November, 1899, at the 23rd *Ghatika i.e.* 2-6 A.M. on the 13th lunar day (*trayodasi*) of the dark half of that month. Between that time and the succeeding new moon day, *i.e.*, two days after that combination a great ruin will come over India. India may not be entirely depopulated or devoured by floods, but famine, pestilence, war and other miseries will reign over the whole country. This is the strong belief and November 1899 is the expected time.

What a firm hold this belief has taken possession of the Hindu mind will become plain to our readers if they refer to the *Madras Mail* of the 24th October last. It will be found there that an astrologer addressed the Dewan in the Mysore Representative Assembly held in October last to make provision for performing *pujas* (worship) to the planets and to propitiate them to avert the impending catastrophe of the year *Vikari* (1899 A. D.), *Kaliyuga* 5000. Some of the members appeared to have been seriously occupied with that matter. The Dewan promised to place the subject before the Maharajah. Eight planets, it is said, according to the astronomical calculations in this country, meet together in November 1899, in the mansion of Scorpio, and not six as the Mysore astrologer stated. Some astrologers say that the meeting of the eight planets is impossible and that only seven meet in one mansion. A Tamil Pandit and astrologer named Mr. Kandaswami Pillai, of Dindigul, in the Madura District, predicted some time ago that the year 1899—Kali 5000—will be one of terrible famine far exceeding that of 1877 in its horrors by reason of the conjunction of the Sun, Mars, Mercury, Venus, Jupiter, Saturn and also the Solar node (*Rahu*) at one and the same sign of the Zodiac Scorpio in November, 1899.

But let us all be more hopeful. The annals of India show a regular series of famines separated by intervals of not more than 3 to 8 years, sometimes 10, and lasting frequently over a year, even as long as three years. The most prolonged famine that India ever experienced was that of 1876-78. The S. W. Monsoon failed in 1875 and 1876. The N. E. Monsoon did not bring in sufficient amount of rain in these years. Between 1876-78 people died in thousands. Whatever the uneducated Hindu may say about the horrors of Kali, these famines must be attributed more to the peculiar position of the mountains in India, especially in the Deccan and Southern India. This interferes with the even distribution of rain. We are fortunately at the end of 1896 A.D. Whatever may be the popular belief about the end of the world in November, 1899, let us only suppose that if any calamity at all is ever to happen as predicted by the *Puranas*, that the years 1897-99 will be a period of prolonged famine as that of 1876-78. Fearing that such may be the case, apart from the puranic ideas, the Government and the charitable public, as would now and then be seen from the columns of the *Madras Mail*, are already adopting measures to avert its evils.

The year 5000 of Kali is the turning point of a minor cycle of 5000 years commencing from Krishna. It is believed by the Occultists that spirituality gains ascendancy after 5000 *Kaliyuga*. It is quite natural to expect such extraordinary events to take place during the time of the change of either major or minor cycle.

APPENDIX B.

Glossary

Ashtami.—The eighth day of a fortnight.

Bhagavad Gita or the Song-Celestial is a dialogue between the hero Arjuna and Krishna who had incarnated upon earth to restore righteousness. It forms Chaps. 25—42 of the Bhishmaparva of the *Mahabharata* and therein are set forth the path of action, the path of devotion, and the path of knowledge, all leading towards one goal, in a manner which is pre-eminently useful to the man of the world engaged in the busiest affairs of life, as to the recluse in the forest.

Bachkanas.—Cloths worn by young children.

Bhavishyottara-purana.—The title of a book—the sacred book which describes the events which are to occur in the future.

Dhoties.—Cloths worn by males.

Dvaraka.—A sacred place in the extreme western projection of the peninsula of Kathiawar, about seven hundred miles to the south-west of Mathura (Muttra) Krishna is Dvarakavasin, one who resides in Dvaraka. It is said that Krishna got the god Visvakarman to build Dvaraka for him on land which the sea bared by receding at his request and the reason assigned for his seeking Dvaraka is that Jarasandha, a king of the Magadhas drove away Krishna and the Yadavas from Mathura.

Ganges.—The river Ganges or Ganga is the mother of Kumara and represents the goddess Vak or Vidya.

Garbagriha.—The Garbagriha is the innermost part of a Hindu Temple, called the holy of the holies. In the Garbagriha the image of the temple god is placed and worshipped.

Gayatri.—The sacred Gayatri verse, to which great religious importance is attached, freely translated means: "Let us meditate as on ourselves, on the shining Creator and All-pervader, that divine light which destroys *avidya* or ignorance and its effects. May that Sun enlighten our intelligence."

This is also the prayer taught to the initiate when he becomes a Brahmana in the Upanayana ceremony, and is used in several rites connected with sacrifices. The verse is repeated many times in the daily Sandhya worships. The sage Visvamitra is supposed to be the author of the Gayatri verse.

Kallan.—A criminal tribe found chiefly in the districts of Madura, Trichinopoly and Tanjore.

Kasan.—A shrub bearing purple flowers, *Memyecylon tinctorium*. Vishnu's colour is said to resemble the colour of Kasan.

Kaveri-snana.—A snana or bath in the river Kaveri. The term Kaveri-snana is applied to fees paid to Brahmans for performing baths in the sacred river Kaveri. The fee thus paid is supposed to wash away the sin of the donor.

Ketaki.—The sweet-scented screwpine flower, *Pandanas oderatissima.*

Navami.—The ninth day of a fortnight.

Philosophy of the Hindus.—There are six schools of Indian philosophy and they are the Nyaya, the Vaisheshika, the Sankhya, the Yoga, the Purva Mimamsa and the Uttara Mimamsa schools. For a good idea of these our readers are referred to Professor Max Müller's excellent treatise on the *Six Systems of Indian Philosophy.*

Rahukala.—An inauspicious portion of the day of the duration of an hour and a half, being that part which is considered to be under the influence of Rahu, the ascending node regarded as one of the nine planets.

Sandhya.—The Sandhya worship in which the Gayatri is used seems to be of very ancient date. The following account is found in the Taittiriya Aranyaka :—

In the old days, the Rakshasas performed hard penances when the god Prajapati asked them as to what boon they wished for. They said in reply : 'Grant that we should fight with the sun' which request the god granted. From that day these Rakshasas are said to be fighting with the rising sun till he sets. But they are put down by means of the water consecrated by uttering the Gayatri. Therefore, these Brahmavadins, facing the east at the morning Sandhya, throw up water consecrated by uttering the Gayatri. The particles of that water become Vajra weapons and throw the Rakshasas down into the island called Mandeharuna. By turning round to the right after throwing up the water, they blow away sin. The Brahman who contemplates the sun at sunrise and sunset and performs Sandhya gets all happiness.

Samudra-snana.—A snana or bath in the sea. This term also like the Kaveri-snana is applied to fees paid to the Brahmans.

Sankalpa.—A solemn vow.

Sari.—A dress consisting of an entire piece of cloth wrapped several times round the loins; and falling down over the legs to the ankle serves as a petticoat. The other end is passed round the neck and hangs on one side.

Sthala-purna.—A purana or legend describing the history of a certain sacred place or temple. It is more mythological than historical.

Sravishta.—The twenty-third lunar mansion consisting of four stars.

Tarka.—Logic.

The Upanishads.—The word Upanishad signifies according to Sri Sankara "that knowledge which tears asunder the veil of ignorance and makes one realise and approach Brahman." It also means "esoteric knowledge or esoteric doctrine" as we find in the Taittiriya Upanishad, Chapter I, 3, "We shall now explain the Upanishad of the Samhita" meaning its esoteric meaning. In the *Mahabharata*, the word Upanishad is used for secret or essence, for when Vyasa speaks of "truth being the Upanishad of the Veda, subjugation of sense, the Upanishad of truth, and charity the Upanishad of the control of the senses," he means that the essence of the Vedas lies in the practice of the influences and that without the latter a knowledge of the Vedas is of no use. Primarily, the word Upanishad therefore means secret knowledge and secondly the books containing that knowledge.

The Upanishads are many in number but the authoritative Upanishads are the Isa, Kena, Katha, Prasna, Munda, Mandukya, Aitreya, Taittireya, Chandogya, Brihadaranyaka and Swetaswatara. The Upanishads are mainly dialogues between teachers and pupils or discussions between sages at king's courts or in the forest. In some cases the gods are declared as imparting knowledge of Brahman to men.

Upanayana.—The performance of Upanayana entitles the Brahmans, the Kshatriyas and Vaisyas to the application of *dvija* twice-born. The ceremony is known as the Upanayana because of the child being carried to or brought near his preceptor for initiation into the Veda. He has his first birth from his natural father and mother but his second birth is from Savitri, the Gayatri as mother, and the preceptor, Acharya, as father. The earliest period for the Upanayana is the seventh or the eighth year for a Brahman, the eleventh for a Kshatriya, and the twelfth for a Vaisya, the latest periods being respectively the 16th, 22nd, and the 24th years after which a *prayaschita* is necessary. The Yagyopavita or sacred thread which the child wears on the day of the Upanayana ceremony consists of three threads and is so called because the person wearing it is invested with the sign of Yagya, another name for Vishnu. The three threads are supposed to represent the three attributes of Satwa, Rajas, and Tamas of which the universe is composed or the three gods Brahma, Vishnu and Siva in one. Its knots represent the *pranava* with the *ardhmatra* and it is worn with the formula: "The Yagyopavita is most sacred; it is the ornament and sign of Brahmanhood. It was produced by Brahma sitting on his seat of lotus and from the threads of the stalk of lotus."

The Vedas.—The Vedas are four in number, *viz.*, the Rig Veda, the Sama Veda, the Yajur Veda and the Atharva Veda. The Rig Veda consists entirely of hymns classified and arranged for worshipping with gratitude and wonder the great and beneficent manifestations and powers of nature. By an ancient custom some of these hymns were chanted in some forms of sacrifice, and a collection of these select hymns, set to music, was called the Sama Veda. Again, special sacrificial formulas were required for the use of the officiating priests, and these formulas were separately collected and known as the Yajur Veda. The Atharva Veda was the last one. The study of the Vedas which were supposed to embody all the learning which it was given to man to acquire, was considered the most important duty and the most cherished heritage of all Hindus.

Vyakarana.– Grammar